Attentive Leadership

Lead with a healthy self-image

Flooris van der Walt

Copyright © 2017 Flooris van der Walt

All rights reserved.

ISBN-13: 978-1979706728

ISBN-10: 1979706727

DEDICATION

I dedicate this book to my wife, Luzell and my two children, Lize and Izak, who through my personal journey of building my self-image, had to put up with me.

Table of Contents

ACKNOWLEDGMENTS	vii
Preface	ix
PART ONE	1
Observations on leadership	3
Tuning my own instrument	19
The journey in authenticity	33
PART TWO	51
Defining the journey	53
Self-awareness	62
Self-evaluation	69
Self-esteem	74
Self-image	82
PART THREE	87
Your journey	89
WORKBOOK	131
Professional identity	136
Partner identity	138
Home Life identity	140
Personality	142
Stage of Life and Career	144
Significant Values	146
Life Networks	148
Health and Fitness	150
BIBLIOGRAPHY	153
ABOUT THE AUTHOR	159

Attentive Leadership

ACKNOWLEDGMENTS

This book and its essence, was born during a Christmas dinner on a boat (what better place to start?), on the beautiful Zurich lake when Franz Killer and I were talking about the fascinating and varying dimensions related to leadership. After explaining to him my leadership concept, which I had for years been incubating and gestating in my head. Franz succinctly responded by saying, "Why don't you write a book on it?" That was the start of a beautiful, inspiring and fascinating journey.

Jurgen Muress and Simon Mitchell have helped tremendously with their reviews and comments on driving the book in the right direction.

Janine Roe has done a marvelous job on not only rewriting the book to better the style, but also to comment on the flow of thought in the book. Thanks Janine. To Sanmarie Hugo and Robby dal Corso, who went with rigor through the proof and made great suggestions and corrections, a big thank you.

I would like to acknowledge all who motivated me to actually finish this book (too many to mention here by name), whether by the simple but considerate act of asking "How is it going?" or by sharing articles and readings which had a connectivity to my book's theme.

Thank you for all this invaluable support. It has carried and inspired me.

Attentive Leadership

Preface

In the current rapidly changing environment, *authenticity* is the only characteristic, as I have discovered, time and again, which will keep you and I intact and allow us to move forward through the inevitable uncertainties and changes we all face on a daily basis.

This book will not only address and concretely confirm the influence of a healthy self-image on leadership, but will also help you and I as leaders, to reflect on our self-image and start the journey on developing a healthier, more wholesome one. This process is however, a lifelong learning process which evolves essentially through the lens of personal reflection.

The book consists of three parts.

At first, I explain the importance of a healthy self-image by using personal examples and reflections which provide a clear understanding of authenticity. Throughout my career in Human Resources, I have constantly received feedback that I am known for connecting well with others. I have come to understand from this feedback that my relationships with others have been more easily and honestly established, as a direct result of my personal authenticity in dealing with others. This is a key factor in the motivation for writing this book and sharing my knowledge and experience with you.

Secondly, I build a model on how self-image is developed and sustained. This will help you and I come to a shared understanding of what exactly it is that I am talking about. Then by extension and progressively, I have endeavored to share with you exactly what the building blocks are in developing a healthy self-image.

Thirdly, I take you, the reader, through a step by step process on precisely *how* our individual self-image can be developed. I hold no mystifying secrets and have been at pains to keep the model as simple as possible. We all however, must remember, that self-image development is a complex process, because our self-image is the sum total of all the combined and multiple experiences we have had in our lives. So, in essence, there is no quick fix, but a life-long commitment to self-awareness and development.

I know from personal experience, that it will be an extremely valuable and helpful asset, to take on the sometimes gargantuan task of reflection with the help of a coach. In the developmental section of my book I strongly recommend that you reflect, together and with the input of others, on how realistic your own self-awareness is, as well as precisely how the gaps between your self-assessment (which may or may not be accurate or realistic) and preferred/desired inner identity can be closed.

This process of realistic and healthy exchange with someone you trust, is crucial, because impartial and mature outsiders are often likely to assess more objectively and can evaluate the global picture and possibly, your situation from a *more neutral* and holistic perspective.

I fervently hope that this book will provide a stimulus to make you, as leaders, aware that your self-image constantly influences others and the way they inevitably respond to you. And that this in turn, affects how your self-image is shaped, going forward.

This book is certainly not designed to delve into pathologies related to self-image. In other words, it is not a discussion on narcissism or any other anti-social personality types, (psychopaths). They are a completely separate and unique field of discussion.

My primary aim here, is to focus on developing a completely attainable, healthy self-image with you, as leaders, who like me, are excited and driven to take up the challenge of developing a more authentic leadership style.

I look forward to sharing the journey with you!

Wohlen AG, Switzerland

PART ONE

Attentive Leadership

Observations on leadership

"I'm sorry Flooris but Jim says we have to move your performance review until after the board meeting."

I have a sense of déjà vu as I hear Jim's PA's words still echoing as I return somewhat dejectedly to my office. This is precisely the same reason given to me previously and I am left feeling puzzled because I know he has completed his midterm review for all my peers. So what gives? What is this actually about?

The first time around I could honestly say that I felt the postponement was reasonable, as I am very well aware that my Chief Executive Officer (CEO) has a lot on his plate. But a second time? I can't help the cascade of questions and doubts rising up in me as I try to make sense of this. Is Jim perhaps trying to tell me something?

Is it that he no longer needs the services of his Head of Group Talent Management? Jim always appears somewhat uncomfortable with awkward situations and maybe he doesn't know how to break the news to me? Or perhaps he is trying to get past the board meeting where I have to present the People Review of the Group and lead the discussions on people capital for a full day with the Board's Human Resources Committee? The uncomfortable thought dawns on me that perhaps he first wants to observe my presentation to the Human Resources Committee before he finalizes his review of my performance. That must be it! My balloon rapidly deflates!

But, as I reflect on the situation, processing the thoughts, images, ideas and anxieties that are flooding through me, I slowly and with more than a little agonizing, grasp that Jim simply is under a great deal of stress and pressure and that the reason he postponed with me and not my peers, is because he knows me well enough to know that I am the one person who will understand his predicament. Well, that's a positive! Sighs inwardly…

These scenarios, where we are confronted with situations that unhinge us, typically play out daily in your and my work environment. Our negative perceptions run amok, as did mine in the above example, and we create an inaccurate picture of an event. If left unchecked – without being subjected to a process of reflection – they are bound to fuel a negative attitude towards our workplace and indeed, our colleagues and principals, and leave us doubting our abilities and ourselves. This will lead to us eventually becoming disengaged, demotivated, disillusioned and frustrated. There is also a knock-on effect which we know, if left unresolved, may result in extreme reaction and actions, and we all know someone who has eventually resigned from the company because they feel aggrieved, injured and unappreciated. We may even have been on that road ourselves and so, intimately understand the effects of situations and work-related matters that somehow derail us emotionally.

In this chapter, I share some general observations on emotions, change, trust, self-image, authenticity and the x–factor in effective leadership. My goal is simply to engage you in thinking about *why* some leaders are effective and others not; and to plant the seed that self-reflection is a powerful tool that can help us to create internal emotional stability in the midst of external turbulence.

Although this particular scenario with Jim played out very recently, in hindsight I can report, that around 20 years ago, I more often than not, began to observe that certain managers in engineering had an excellent connection and relationship with their employees, whereas others were falling far short of this vital link in the corporate chain. I had no choice but to ask myself why this was the case and what the contributing factors were. What is that magic, elusive ingredient that separates one group from the other? And indeed, is there a practical solution one way or the other, to *make it better*, more fruitful an exercise, for that group which struggles, and even for those who seemingly manage effortlessly, to still improve?

My observation led me to an interesting hypothesis. It is an intriguing but very relevant fact, that the same part of our brain which stimulates the creation and appreciation of classical music also plays an integral role in the complexities of mathematics. I therefore hypothesized that people who have an appreciation and understanding of classical and other music, (which we all know stimulates and stirs the emotions), may *also* possess the ability to be outstanding mathematicians. An epiphany of sorts? Perhaps you have reached the same conclusion and certainly anecdotal evidence concerning one of science's giants supports my hypothesis. I read the following comment in the HuffPost with great interest; David H Bailey and Jonathan M Borwein (2017) give historical evidence:

> "Perhaps the best real-life example of a mathematician-musician was Albert Einstein, who, as many who knew him personally would attest, was also an accomplished pianist and violinist. His second wife Elsa told of how Albert, while during deep concentration on a mathematical problem, would sit down at the piano and play for a while; after one two-week period, interspersed with random piano playing, Einstein emerged the first working draft of general relativity. He once said, "If ... I were not a physicist, I would probably be a musician. I often think in music. I live my daydreams in music. I see my life in terms of music."

This is just one example of many who fit the mould of mathematical genius and musical giftedness.

The only obvious conclusion I can come to therefore, is that those people who are inclined towards and gifted in the sciences (mathematics and engineering for instance), must logically also possess the ability to be emotionally sensitive. For me, this was pretty amazing and liberating stuff!

It dawned on me then that herein might lie an important clue and key factor in defining the *difference* between the two *types* of managers in engineering I described earlier. The one group is sensitive and emotionally well balanced. This group is able to integrate these dimensions wisely with practical issues and is therefore able to also deal with human fragilities and sensitivities and not only technical managerial issues. If you belong to this group, you will tend to flow easily with emotions and their effect on the people you lead.

The second group focuses only on the typical engineer-mindset, which is less comfortable with the emotional issues. This group has a real struggle in dealing with the human and abstract nature of their co-workers and employees and indeed, their own flawed and sometimes unpredictable emotions. If you belong to the second group, then the world of emotions may not be your *happy place*. You are inclined to see emotional issues as daunting and often inexplicable. Your interpretation and processing of emotional aspects, will, indubitably, affect the outcomes of each and every leadership situation you find yourself in and the very critical influence you have on your colleagues and employees.

If you find yourself relating to the second group, you may understandably feel threatened by these apparently non-quantifiable issues within yourself and your employees, and may struggle to de-code and understand the manifestations thereof. It is this unknown dimension – the emotional aspect – which often unsettles our equilibrium as leaders. The *how to* deal with people, partners, employees and even ourselves in the emotional arena is a pervasive challenge and issue that looms large and may at times, unhorse us on our walk-through life.

So often, in the 30 years I have worked in Industry, have I heard these words uttered: "You have to understand… I am an engineer!" This has been presented as a standard defense from leaders. When faced with this loaded response, I have always wondered, exactly, what does this mean? What is this person really saying to me? Is it an excuse? When I use the term *excuse*, I can't but wonder if this kind of retort is an exercise in escape and evasion from having to acknowledge that emotions are an uncomfortable part of work and leadership.

I completely acknowledge that not everyone is equally equipped to deal with emotions, but whether we like it or not, emotions are a large part of who we are as humans, those *interesting beings who inhabit this planet*. This applies whether we are the sort who are open about expressing and acknowledging emotion, or whether we are inclined to mask and hide our true feelings. These so-called *un-knowns* are an essential part of the world we connect to as leaders. Making room for the role emotions play in our inner world and external environment, is an inescapable part of life. By extension therefore, it goes without saying, that building relationships and trust, and connecting with others is an element we cannot ignore, and that involves… no prizes for guessing… emotion!

The building of relationships and trust is an essential part of life but more specifically in the context we are addressing, forms the base for effective leadership. If we are not prepared to deal with or allow our emotions a degree of visibility, we are sure to struggle with insight of self and others, and the net effect is that we will inevitably be poor managers and leaders. This I say because I have seen it happen countless times in my years of experience in Human Resources. And if we are to be candid with ourselves, we will acknowledge that we have all seen it play out in our personal encounters with leaders, and with managers.

This hypothesis and journey which strives to make sense of and understand how our emotions affect whether or not we are being more productive people and leaders, is what has driven my keen observations during the many years I have spent in industry. I have come to the realization too, that learning to work with your emotions is a highly desirable goal, not only when it comes to engineers but that it ideally, should be applied to a wide range of leaders, and include those who are in the fields of human science, natural science, chemistry and other disciplines.

We have all observed leaders, who are like the first group of engineers I alluded to earlier, who appear to bond and connect with their employees in an apparently seamless and natural way. Through my therapeutic application and experiences, I have been able to understand these behaviors and make sense of the rationale driving them. Even so I have also persistently sought to deepen my understanding of emotions and emotional connectedness in leadership and asked myself, "What tools can be used to enhance and improve these very relevant qualities that make one a better leader?" In this quest, I have persistently questioned which factors contribute to the fact that some leaders are more efficient in leading both themselves and their employees with such ease and flow, and why others struggle to connect with people and as a consequence are less able to influence them in a positive way.

I explored this pressing question when working on my second Master's thesis in the theme of "Strategic Behavior of Transformational Leaders", but it still remained a mystery as to what the key factors were that formed the difference between these two categories of leaders. The one group effortlessly takes their employees on the journey with them, and the other group often tries extremely hard, but does not succeed in leading and influencing their subordinates and others for the global good.

A reasonable conclusion I came to, as presented in my Thesis (van der Walt, 1994) could be that the different leadership styles dependent on the foundation of a certain level of emotional maturity which you, the leader, would employ to guide your behavior. This, combined with your inherent personality traits, (e.g. to what extent you compensate for your weaknesses by getting those on your team to actively co-operate and contribute their inherent strengths) will ensure that this combined effort yields far more fruitful outcomes than that of you as an individual flying solo. We simply can't go it alone… All in all, this has added to my understanding of the role of emotion in leadership.

But still, further questions arise. Why do we find so many cases of emotionally immature behavior amongst our leaders? Do you and I operate from a level of inner confidence and security or do we flounder in our own self-doubt and insecurity? Is this linked to the million-dollar solution where we more easily facilitate the process of necessary change, and do you and I utilize our inherent *strengths and weaknesses* to initiate and guide our personal process of maturation? These are questions we should all be asking of ourselves.

As a further observation, emotional maturity, as a basic but vital requirement for effective leadership, has not changed much throughout the challenges I have witnessed since writing my theses until the present time. Having said this, I do believe the complexity and speed with which change and flux is occurring has dramatically increased through the years. This rapid change creates even more potential for leadership derailment and emotional immaturity, and according to my way of thinking, emotional maturity is the critical differentiator in dealing successfully with rapid change and complexities which exist in the present-day world.

I have also observed that leaders among us who are able to motivate and centralize people around the same goal or objective, have not necessarily had to use extreme formulae and complicated systems to analyze what the needs are in any given situation, nor did they necessarily consciously behave in a certain way in specific situations. For those of you who operate this way, it has been more a matter of common sense on what to do and how to behave – it is almost an automatic response – and the process is… authentic! Herein lies the clue, and it is key!

Harvard Business Review of November 2011 published a great story.

The *story* developed like this and points to further clues in understanding what leaders need in order to be effective; self-reflection and self-disclosure.

Clynton, the managing director of a large German beauty corporation, was exhausted by the passive culture in his company. Everyone depended on him and avoided hard decisions. He wanted his senior managers to take more initiative. It took a 360° review to show him that his directive leadership style was a big part of the problem. He could have worked in private to change his behavior - but instead he stood up at an annual meeting of his top 60 managers, acknowledged his failings, and outlined both his personal and his organizational goals. He admitted that he didn't have all the answers and asked his team for help in leading the company. By exposing himself in this way, he set a standard - and an agenda - for others to follow. Clynton said:

> "I shared with my team the kind of leader I aspired to be. I asked every member to hold me accountable to that vision. This set an expectation that each of them would mirror my commitment."

"As more people got on board, the momentum increased. Over the next two years Clynton became very adept at using silence and open-ended questions to encourage his team to step up. His effectiveness surged, and his team flourished; dependent behaviors gave way to initiative and innovation, and his organization has outperformed much larger competitors in the six years since" (Fuda and Badham, 2011). He describes it like this:

> "Soon we added more layers of leadership to the process, all accountable to one another regardless of our position in the hierarchy. It felt like a massive snowball rolling down the hill, with me trapped in the middle."

What is the x-factor? What is it about leaders like Clynton, and what qualities do they possess, which enable them to almost effortlessly galvanize their employees around accomplishing a shared goal, and in so doing effect the necessary actions and changes required in a given situation, project or assignment? Based on my observations, I learned that the one trait which truly stands out in my estimation is *trust*.

At this point I would ask you to pause and take a moment to reflect on this quality. The conclusion I arrived at is a by-product of much deliberation and reflection, and I will go as far as to say that people who evoke trust, will more naturally and comfortably hold a large sphere of influence. This is seen in action when employees seem likely to go to any lengths to please and *follow the leader*, if you will. I am not talking about *blind*, or *unconditional* trust, with its obvious pitfalls. I am talking about trust that makes followers feel safe in the presence of and under the direction of their leaders.

This may seem glaringly obvious, but think on this. There simply has to be that fertile ground, where people *feel* or *sense* that the person in charge (leader, for formal purposes) is genuine and worthy of their trust, and that they feel *safe* with the leader. Time and again it has been seen that when people experience a healthy degree of trust in the person in charge, they go to great lengths to support and assist the person, and they are faithful in their attitude towards the leader and the assignments delegated to them.

When I googled the meaning of authenticity, I got the following:

"Truthfulness of origins, attributions, commitments, sincerity, and intentions".

These are what I believe to be the attributes such leaders need in order to build trusting relationships with employees and in so doing, get the snowball rolling!

Gradually over time, I have come to the realization that all of my *discoveries* around emotion, self-reflection, self-disclosure, trust and emotional maturity can be rolled up into one concept: Authenticity. Authenticity is the x-factor in leadership and can only really be achieved on the foundation of a *well-developed healthy self-image* which is supported by a good self-esteem and which, through time, has been molded by self-awareness and reflection. (We will revisit this formula at a later stage in the book.) In concluding this chapter, I would like to share some thoughts and views on self-image and self-esteem for you to reflect on.

In the process of developing a self-image profile for adults, Butler and Gasson (2006) recognized that a positive self-concept is central to adaptive behavior. A high degree of self-esteem is associated with greater autonomy, a sense of mastery, positive relationships with others and self-acceptance. These are hallmarks of authentic leaders who thus lead change in an integrated and uncontrived, natural way.

Tracy (2014) wrote that self-esteem is simply how much you like yourself and that an important part of self-esteem is self-efficacy. It is a feeling of competence, of being good at what you are doing and having the ability to delegate to others what you are not good at, while at the same time being confident that those to whom you have delegated assignments to are competent to successfully carry them out diligently. Making the distinction between who is competent or gifted in which specific area, is only possible when you have a vivid and clear understanding of yourself, in addition a healthy self-image is paramount. This is the trademark of an effective leader and is sure to produce fruitful results.

Having said this, the extreme is not beneficial either. This is what CEO Cheryl Bachelder (2015) from Popeyes Louisiana Kitchen restaurants describes, "Many leaders see themselves as the star of the show. These spotlight leaders are self-centered. Their attitude derives from authority-based leadership; they describe their vision, provide all the answers and show their employees the way to go. These leaders demand attention and affirmation. They use their power and authority to make others do their bidding and seldom bring out the best in the people who work for them."

She offers an alternative: her "Dare-to-Serve"-leadership is all about acting with confidence, to help your employees to believe that they can achieve goals beyond self-serving ambitions. Cheryl's employees create personal purpose statements which help define their values and identify their strengths. The result of the turnaround at Popeye's Louisiana Kitchen was, for me, captured in the statement, "Respect people and protect their dignity without regard to their rank or achievements." This can only be brought about in the capable hands of a leader with a healthy self-image.

Logically then, a healthy self-image creates a platform for exploring the influence that this desirable quality has on the authenticity of the leader. Authenticity in turn, is a vital catalyst in effecting smooth change, flux and response to change within the organization, especially in a rapidly fluctuating environment in our present day.

"Roughly one-third of the firms on Fortune magazine's annual list of the best 100 companies to work for, say that they 'intentionally practice servant leadership'. Servant leadership requires ongoing professional and personal growth. Servant leaders are eager to broaden their knowledge, and they're open to learning opportunities." (Tenney, 2014).

In the following part of this book, I shall endeavor to relate to you the influence of *self-image* in everyday examples. Around these illustrations I build on concepts which you will find to be conducive to developing a healthy self-image. When this dynamic prevails and actively manifests, you, the leader, will be better able to lead your employees in an environment which is vastly less stressful. You won't feel as though you are *faking it* and the risk of burn-out and surrendering to the pressures involved will be enormously diminished.

The exciting news for you and I really, is that we don't have to be enmeshed by complicated situations which consume us in a negative way. That, simply put, as I will demonstrate in the chapters ahead, comes about as a direct result of being *authentic*!

Tuning my own instrument

In this chapter I would like to provide you with some insights into how some of the key concepts I discussed in the previous chapter were woven into my life and helped me to become more authentic. I also expound on the importance of self-image in leadership and leadership development.

Certainly, for a good part of my career, I was like an out of tune violin. Playing all the right notes on an out of tune instrument can only produce a discordant sound. My journey towards greater authenticity was much like tuning a violin. The tuning pegs had to be turned, the strings had to be stretched, then the pegs had to be turned again and the strings stretched some more. The process is one of trial and error before the correct pitch is obtained and is not without screeching and popping sounds as the instrument is progressively brought into tune!

I am the second-born son in a family of four children. From the beginning, I was always somewhat different to my siblings. I was the only one of the four who went to university after finishing school and I drove myself hard in order to be successful. I have often wondered what the source of this drive has been, taking into account too, that neither of my parents went on to tertiary education.

Interestingly, there have been quite a number of friends and acquaintances who have had a tremendous influence in my life, but one in particular, said something to me one day. What he said stopped me dead in my tracks! Something very important dawned on me when he ironically exclaimed,

> "Flooris, you remind me of a Christmas tree, decorated with all your degrees and, you know something? It doesn't even look good!"

At this point in my academically charged life, I had completed my sixth degree with two of them on a Master's Level. To say that I was flabbergasted by his comment was an understatement of note and I was shaken to the core! I had been studying for 13 years in total, with five of those as a full-time student and the balance part-time.

His keen observation woke me up from a *reverie* of sorts, as I realized that I had been striving intensely to over-compensate for my low self-image! I was trying to become an expert in learning so many different compositions and practicing my heart out to be the best violinist, but the reality was that my instrument was completely out of tune. What emerged in that moment was extreme discomfort as the conductor interrupted the whole orchestra mid-stride in order for me to attend to the discordant sounds emanating from me! The rehearsal was halted while I had to attend to my tuning exercise! Not my most comfortable experience!

This was a significant and pivotal moment for me as my friend's feedback truly gave me a fresh insight. Thus began my own journey, to re-create my self-image and try to build my fledgling self-esteem. This I realized, would require careful nurturing until an intact and healthy self-image emerged that could stand on its own two feet!

The process I embarked upon was one of countless ups and downs. That in itself allowed me to immerse myself fully in the journey, while endeavoring to reflect and ask for feedback from those close to me. This was a vital step in discovering who I really was, what I was particularly good at and what areas to develop. I reflected on what I was not happy with or prepared to do or invest in? This process of self-evaluation, where I continuously confronted myself with these central questions, incrementally afforded me more internal security and constructed a base from which I could keep my self-esteem stable and in balance.

I can closely identify with Malley (2014) who said, "You won't get anywhere shying away from failure, mistakes, rejection or other adversity. Regard difficulties as catalysts for growth. They provide opportunities to learn new skills, toughen your resilience and boost your self-confidence. To reach your goals, step out of your comfort zone and replace fear with passion, authenticity, confidence and patience." Certainly, I had to persevere through many trials, times of despondency and pressures from all sides, as I progressed on my journey to develop an accurate understanding of who I am. The violin strings were stretched again and again!

In order to unravel the background to understand where my need for compensation arose, I reflected with my mother on the canvas of my early childhood and the pictures that my early experiences painted on it. (As I am a Jungian therapist I realize the importance of the developmental phases in life.) She related to me that my father only once visited her in hospital after the event of my birth! He was apparently deeply disappointed that I hadn't been the daughter he so desperately wanted.

This underlying rejection, of which I was not even consciously aware during my childhood, was very likely a contributing reason why my attempts at building a relationship with my father were hamstrung time and again. Needless to say, in summary, that the disconnected relationship with my father during the course of my life had a very direct influence on how I felt about myself and it shaped my self-image in a profound way. And so, going forward in my life, I repeated less than healthy patterns to compensate for this lack – in my particular case, trying to fill the void by becoming the proverbial *Christmas tree*, hung with academic achievements in the shape of degrees. A broken, out of tune violin attempting valiantly to do justice to Bach, Beethoven, Mozart, Tchaikovsky…

After the watershed encounter with my friend, I decided to cease all formal studies and begin to seriously focus on my own development as a person, and in particular, my self-awareness. This I did privately, and in conjunction with close, trusted friends. This was not only an exciting journey but also a very real time of exploration, of testing my limits and constantly evaluating what I liked and did not like. In short, what made my motors run, and what made me want to run in the opposite direction? Throughout this process I constantly tested my inner person and asked all the hard and uncomfortable questions.

The experiences which were created by this process made me feel good about myself for periods which stretched longer and longer over time. An evolution gradually took shape where I could look at myself in a more balanced way. My improved perspective gave rise to building a self-image which could properly support me in my career and relationships.

This was no quick sprint I will tell you! It was more like an endurance marathon at times, because there are no overnight cures when self-development is at work. I had to learn how to believe in myself, how to evaluate my strengths and weaknesses and reflect privately. With the help of friends and coaches, I had to build a realistic awareness of whether I was the classical violin or whether I inclined more towards the Flamenco Guitar! Who is the man, Flooris? A happy result of this introspective journey was that I learned better how to trust myself, and that I could evaluate my behaviors and feelings in a holistic and realistic manner.

At the same time, it was sometimes a challenge to make peace with and accept that others would get to know me more intimately; the good, the bad and the ugly. I had to define the *good* Flooris, (my positive attributes and characteristics) whilst acknowledging the *evil twin* (my weaknesses). I knew I had to compensate for my areas of weakness but also, to make peace with them, and more importantly, manage them in a way that was constructive and not destructive. I would like to say at this juncture, that *making peace* and *being resigned* are not the same thing. I could choose to *resign myself* to the attributes that were less than helpful and so continue stubbornly in negative patterns, or I could *make peace* with my areas of development but still embrace opportunities to work towards a more *whole* and integrated me.

Slowly, painstakingly, but surely this instrument was being tuned – my self-image and awareness of who I am was taking shape. I knew that I was far from being a Stradivarius yet, but I was bent on being as close to emulating that iconic masters' instrument as was humanly possible!

As I got to know myself more intimately and reflected on my understanding of my feelings and behaviors, together with others, I became better equipped to gain a clearer picture of the ways in which I was perceived by others. That offered the *potential* for me to establish a healthy self-image, where I could confidently believe in my abilities and capabilities and thus illuminating future possibilities in my life! This, I firmly believe, was the foundation on which I have managed a successful and sustainable international career.

Start tuning

Why do I give self-image so much air-time? It is because our behavior is an extension of our self-image. This behavior is observed and experienced by others in the workplace, at business gatherings, conferences, in meetings and when interacting with family and friends, and provides them with a window into your consolidated self-image and by extension how you perceive yourself in any given situation.

Ask yourself, "How do I handle pressurized situations? Do I exude confidence when addressing a problem? How do I tackle those common and uncomfortable situations? Do I trust in my ability to draw on my particular competencies when I deal with people? Am I comfortable in understanding and evaluating situations, and do I speak up when I do not understand all the aspects related? Am I secure in the knowledge that I can draw from previous experience and personal knowledge to resolve matters?

Behavior is a multi-faceted place, and the degree to which all elements within you harmoniously delivers the musical allegory, depends heavily on just how healthy your self-image is and how well you take care to keep this instrument in tune.

As far back as 1964, the Harvard Business Review wrote an article on "The Power to See Ourselves". This article clearly states that management development (today it is dubbed leadership development) means change in a person's self-concept. This article drives home the point that each of us, whether we give it credence or not, possess a unique self-image - we all see ourselves in some way – smart, slow, kindly, well-intentioned, lazy, misunderstood, meticulous, or shrewd (Brouwer, 1964). This in turn affects the way we relate to and lead others and how others relate back to us and the extent to which they would be willing to follow our lead. In a nutshell, it drives our behavior. I would argue then that this would be the focal point from which to start Leadership Development. Developing a healthy self-image is, and should be, the basis from which to contemplate and construct any form of Leadership Development, and is indeed, a weighty challenge!

Not only is self-image the engine room of behavior, it is also your personal anchor in the face of turbulence. In developing leaders whose leadership skills are sure to have fruitful impact and who are transformational, we are also faced with the undeniable fact that the future is an unknown. The future cannot be perfectly planned, designed or structured. It is a state where there is no security, no safety net, no schedule or manual to exactly define how you are to deal with the unknown. This is a no-brainer to us all but it is very helpful to be mindful of this reality and prepare ourselves accordingly.

However, we have the potential to develop self-knowledge and an awareness of what we are intrinsically capable of and how we can compensate for those things we realistically know are not our strengths. This is self-image at its core and people with a clear and well understood knowledge of themselves can use this as an anchor to maintain internal stability even when the external environment is turbulent. It is the ingredient that will guide and lead you and your team through the inevitable phases of change and uncertainty.

Tuning authentically

So far, I have explained in my personal journey how I came to the realization that in order to be authentic, I needed to focus on getting to know myself and on developing my self-image. I have also argued that this is the compass point where leadership development should start. I hope by this stage, it is patently obvious, that by developing this deeper self – knowledge and awareness you and I will be well able to equip ourselves to lead effectively in an uncertain and unstable environment. Heraclitus, the Greek philosopher, once said, "Change is the only constant". This certainly helps put things in perspective.

It is interesting to reflect on the psycho-neurological dimensions of change.

Swart, Chisholm and Brown (2015) explain it this way:

> "Leaders change themselves, too. Your brain changes constantly as you make new connections among neurons. For

substantial change, these connections have to be "robust" enough to disrupt established habits. You must apply "focused attention" to harness your brain's energy use. . . Change is easier in an environment that supports your actions."

The purpose of this effort is to establish a healthy and realistic self-image (in psychological terminology: "to build ego strength") by systematically engaging in a process of self-development. This will create authenticity and bring you into harmonious alignment with yourself, and thereby enable you to inspire others to be more integrated, authentic leaders; leaders who are at the core, honest with themselves. This applies whether you are a leader in business, politics, sport, an association or in your own personal space.

I have made several references in this book to the current world we live in and the constant change we are faced with. A world where the future is unpredictable and everyone is uncertain of what to expect. And indeed, how to deal with the changes. Stable leadership is sorely needed in this turbulent environment. This is why I repeatedly emphasize, that it is of paramount importance that we begin, and continue, to look inwardly at who we really are, what we can and cannot do well, and come to grips with our personal strengths and weaknesses. This will provide us with a stable inner compass and also give us the confidence to allow others to do what we can't; to compensate for our shortcomings without feeling threatened or inadequate. This is the leader you and I need and want to be, someone with the inner stability to understand, manage, deal with and influence complex situations in a productive way. A way in which the least amount of *damage control* surfaces. When our core is fragile or an unquantifiable factor within ourselves, we are vulnerable and can easily be derailed by the turbulent winds of change and uncertainty.

To reiterate, we want to be leaders who are *authentic* and who can be trusted to deliver what we promise and action, sometimes in the face of rejection and lack of co-operation. We are not going to win all the popularity contests, let's face it. But I can't help smiling as an image comes to mind; it is better to be a person with a difficult personality, someone who is rude and small-minded, to whom others will eventually adjust and become accepting, however grudgingly, than trying to please everybody and change behavior and direction like the wind and the world changes. This only confuses people and destroys trust!

Authentic leaders are valued over insincerity. Some might be more unpleasant than other. It is however easier to relate to a known unpleasant personality than a fake on-off pretense.

Tuning fake behaviors

Allow me to expound somewhat on this last statement as I don't want anyone to misunderstand my meaning. I have come to fully believe that there exists a significant gap in training leaders in terms of *behavior modification*. For example, think about common training themes such as "how to give feedback", "how to conduct an evaluation discussion", "how to motivate your employees", and other similar concepts which may be considered here. These behavioral training topics are *handles* which are designed to help leaders have guide ropes to hold onto while dealing with and leading people. Unfortunately these behaviors are *learned* and most of the time, in my experience, the *learned behavior* has been so poorly integrated into and aligned with the leader's authentic self that the expression thereof comes across as *phony*, and *contrived*.

Real-time examples you may have experienced are the typical ones where a particular manager returns from a *leadership* motivational training course, and duly shakes the hands of his employees with what sounds suspiciously like a scripted comment such as: "I know you can do it!" or "I trust in your abilities". The recipient of such generous praise might wonders why the sudden change in behavior, because he is known to be the most controlling, micro-managing individual, who always checks on your every move, decision and any iota of correspondence that leaves his department – and all that until only last week? Did said manager suddenly undergo a metamorphosis to become the real deal? Most people can be forgiven for wondering whether this manager is to be trusted because his behavior is suddenly so incongruent with historical evidence and you fear that aliens have abducted his body and sold it to the gypsies! So, there, the *trust* word becomes relevant again.

People quickly sense behavior which is not authentic, and hence trustworthiness is not engendered. You will quickly discern whether mannerisms and *speak* emanates from the *real* manager who frustrated you the previous week, or whether the *true unpleasantness* will resurface by the end of next week!

So, in essence, you and I as leaders, are compelled to look at ourselves in totality as opposed to reviewing isolated examples. Do we walk the talk of learned and discordant behavior or the talk of authenticity and consistency? Are we sounding *in tune* to the hearer or recipient or do they wince inwardly when they hear the screech of the violin string? Learned behavior which is not authentically integrated will not be understood or appreciated by your employees and they will pick up on any inconsistency, of that you can be sure. It will help you immensely if you remind yourself of this on your journey.

It is for this very reason that my argument supports starting with the core of who we are. In the realm of sojourning and executing meaningful leadership development, that core has proved to function well in the arena of a healthy self-image; one which is built on self-awareness, private and assisted self-reflection. Our instrument - our authentic self - should be properly in tune so that we easily play in harmony with the rest of the orchestra…and that we don't jar the ear of the listener.

I will deal with this construct in more detail later in the book.

Attentive Leadership

The journey in authenticity

We touched briefly on how we can establish authenticity earlier in the book and I also shared some of my own journey in establishing greater authenticity. In this chapter I would like to explore the theme of authenticity in greater detail.

Authenticity in behavior

Let's revisit the manager who unexpectedly enters your personal space, a little too close for comfort, shakes your hand and now appears, miraculously, to be the supreme motivator, exclaiming as he delegates an assignment to you…

"I know you can do it!"

With this exclamation, he appears convinced that he has been magically transformed into an authority and guru on how to motivate his employees! However, your thought processes are reeling and your thought bubble reads,

"Where on earth is he coming from all of a sudden?"

You sense a distinct disconnect. You don't recognize him because his behavior is so out of character and you are also very mindful of the fact that this particular manager hasn't had a clue about your actual capabilities up until this point. He has neglected to give you any clear guidance on how to carry out this assignment prior to this moment. Worse still, he has not yet proven that he knows how to get the desired result that he expects from you! In a nutshell, he doesn't know whether *you can, in fact, do it*, and hasn't *dialed in* to assess what guidance to give you to meet his expectation. The entire experience screams "fake!"

You happen to know that your newly enthusiastic manager recently learned a few tricks in the motivational workshop he attended, such as "how to interact meaningfully with others", and now he is doing his level best to practice and impress his new skills on everyone on his path! This kind of behavior meets with disbelief from employees, as they innately sense, that he is not being real. Perhaps he would have been more effective if he had just been his recognizable self.

Of course, I am not discounting the manager's enthusiasm or motivation. But, in trying to fulfill the brief he has done nothing to first establish his authenticity with you. A more credible alternative for this particular manager would be to sit down with you, plan the course ahead, define detailed milestones, and where necessary, admit that he doesn't have all the answers and that your co-operative effort may be the best strategy going forward! You will certainly feel more assured, and appreciate that he is being real, *authentic* and you will be far more willing to be motivated by him because you now know the true lay of the land, where he stands, and where you fit in with his expectations.

The *behavior modification* business has developed into a multi-billion-dollar industry. Its aim is to educate leaders on how to behave. Typical themes taught are: "How to motive your employees", "How to give feedback", and "How to empower others". Very often, however, this training results in managers assuming roles of prescribed and learned behaviors which are inconsistent with their inherent and true selves. They have not integrated these techniques with their core and self-image. This inevitably results in the manager coming across as *phony*, inappropriate and even insincere. One and one don't add up to two and you are left with a sense of applied gimmicks rather than genuine and authentic engagement.

I have personally observed how employees will accept and follow leaders who perhaps have, shall we say, *difficult* personalities, but who are genuine in their interaction with others, often to the point of defending such a manager. Why is this? It is very simply because there is a marked consistency in the manager's behavior and style, and employees orientate themselves with this dynamic and adjust their internal responses to his management style. At the heart of it, they observe and experience a certain authenticity at work. In a nutshell, they come to terms with and accept to a degree, challenging aspects related to their manager's personality traits, and they do so because the manager is truly authentic and genuine. This authenticity seems to inspire a level of loyalty and trust.

In the Harvard Business Review of November 2011, the following story was published and provides a powerful example of the effects of inauthentic versus authentic leadership on followers and organizational performance.

> "I felt ill prepared for my promotion to such a big job, so I tried to bluff my way through. I thought, "Okay, I will be the tough guy. It's working for my boss; he's scaring the hell out of me." But this didn't work, so I tried a different approach: "I'll be the nice guy. 'Thank you for saying thank you!'" That didn't work either. I was guessing and making it up as I went along. I was a bit of a fake" (Fuda and Badham, 2011).

The story unfolded as follows,

> "Mike, the CEO of a multinational IT outsourcer, had a very difficult first three months in his job. The company's financial results were poor, and his credibility was being called into question. It quickly became clear that Mike himself was a major cause of the problems. His inconsistent behavior meant that his colleagues wasted energy trying to second-guess him. He

realized that he would need to drop the imitations and rebuild his leadership identity. That meant focusing on his core business values, fairness and accountability, along with values he'd previously reserved for his family, such as empathy and connection. Once Mike started behaving more authentically at work, his team began to engage with him in increasingly positive ways, and his superiors became more trusting and supportive. Over the next five years Mike's leadership effectiveness ratings soared, and the company's profits more than tripled" (Fuda and Badham, 2011).

The inevitable question now arises:

How do we bring a manager who initially behaves like Mike, to the realization that although being *authentic* may not necessarily put him in a position where he seems to have all the answers or equip him to solve all future problems, he will nevertheless have a more positive effect on others? Authenticity brings with it a degree of vulnerability, but paradoxically, as we see with Mike, it is this vulnerability that made him more effective. As he consciously evaluated his behavior and the effect it had on his employees, he was able to connect better with his team by being real and authentic. When a manager is authentic, employees will see him as being more open, more in touch with himself, secure in knowing his strengths and weaknesses and therefore able to deal with development areas within himself effectively and constructively.

Authenticity and self-disclosure

Having said this, it is noteworthy that we all possess hidden or private areas. This is not at all a bad thing and I am not suggesting that all leaders should expose themselves to the extent that private matters are open for all to inspect. Rosh and Offermann (2013) warn that too much openness at work might be dangerous,

> "… the honest sharing of thoughts, feelings, and experiences at work is a double-edged sword: "Despite its potential benefits, self-disclosure can backfire if it's hastily conceived, poorly timed, or inconsistent with cultural or organizational norms - hurting your reputation, alienating employees, fostering distrust, and hindering teamwork. Getting it right takes a deft touch, for leaders at any stage of their careers."

Each of us need to decide for ourselves what we are comfortable in revealing to employees or the public at large. Leaders are logically more *visible* so to speak, but being *authentic* doesn't translate into you having to bare your soul in public. It means simply, that it is beneficial to create an environment where people understand where you stand on matters, and how you think and feel about specific situations and ideas. You want others to be able to read you accurately and not be left in doubt as to who you are and what you are about.

From my experience, selectively keeping information about yourself private doesn't mean that it will hinder you from being a leader who is authentic. Personal privacy should not be confused with openness and authentic expression.

This point is illustrated by my earlier reference to authors (Rosh and Offermann, 2013) who recognize that, "Authenticity begins with self-awareness; knowing who you are — your values, emotions, and competencies — and how you're perceived by others. Only then can you know what to reveal and when."

If your *words* integrates harmoniously with your *actions*, your viewpoints and stance on matters in the workplace are more likely to be correctly interpreted by those around you. When people experience you as being consistently authentic and honest, the effect will be felt in the prevalent culture of your work environment. I have seen how interpersonal relationships prosper when this dynamic is at the fore.

Authenticity as your reference point

It is widely understood that we are all imperfect and this is inherently accepted by most in the workplace. Imperfection does not negate authenticity. Exhibiting authenticity does not mean that we will lose the respect of our employees and colleagues. People lose respect for you when they cannot get a *handle* on who you are, or when your behavior is erratic and inconsistent, and when they never know what to expect from you. Not only do they lose respect, they lose interest. Your framework or reference point from which you lead others should not entail the latest behavior modification tricks and techniques which you learnt at a seminar; the *artificial* behavior which I referred to earlier in chapter one. The only position from which to develop a stable and authentic pattern of relating to others, is to use the real you as your reference point and build from there.

I fully agree with Brené Brown (2010) who says it is so much easier to respond with,

> "I'll be whoever or whatever you need me to be, as long as I feel like I'm part of this",

than to be our authentic selves. We as humans have the desire and need to belong. We generally want to fit in with our colleagues and be successful in our respective careers. That is normal. We want to be able to fulfil our supervisor's expectations. Circumstances and situations do not automatically pan out perfectly however, and often we find ourselves alienated and not belonging. The reason for this might be that which Brené states wisely,

> "We can only belong when we offer our most authentic selves and when we're embraced for who we are."

Effort and deliberate intent are required to bring about this status quo.

In a Harvard Business Review article Herminia Ibarra (2015) comments on her research that she observed how career advancements require all of us to move way beyond our comfort zones. The challenge becomes apparent when we stretch ourselves to depart from that comfort zone, because a strong counter-impulse is triggered in order to protect our identities. This often translates into a lack of confidence and a feeling of being unsure of ourselves or of our ability to perform well or measure up in a new setting. As a result, we often retreat to familiar behaviors and styles.

When we scrutinize our reactions to these situations, the thoughts and emotions that direct them and how they impact on and are perceived by others, we find ourselves in the forge of developing a sustainable self-image. This can be a challenging process, but it will help us to transition to a place where we can authentically deal with the new challenges before us. The alternatives to this are getting stuck in old behavior patterns that do not match up with the new requirements, or to use *clip-on behavior modification techniques* that make us recognizably plastic and fake. I will explain more about this in the second part of the book

Ibarra also makes a profound point in saying that the moments which most challenge our sense of self are the ones that can teach us the most about leading effectively. While these moments may make us feel vulnerable we need not fear them if we accept that our development is an ongoing journey. "By viewing ourselves as works in progress and evolving our professional identities through trial and error, we can develop a personal style that feels right to us and suits our organizations' changing needs" (Ibarra, 2015).

When we are unsuccessful in developing our professional identity and personal style, based on our experiences and reflection on our reactions to them, we run the risk of becoming straight-jacketed, sometimes with devastating consequences.

I am reminded of my first manager, who I will call Viktor, when I first moved to Switzerland. He believed that we should never mix professional and personal relationships. This meant that although we had known one another personally and interacted socially before my appointment, now that I was reporting to him, we had to put that behind us and could only engage on a professional level. This new set of circumstances threw our relationship into a disequilibrium of sorts and he was clearly uncomfortable with transitioning to this dual relationship. It pushed him out of his comfort zone, and instead of being willing to work though this painful process and find a new equilibrium he opted to put rigid boundaries around our relationship. In his mind, this would be an effective way to deal with the now blurred personal/professional boundaries in our relationship.

I only understood his reasoning and behavior many years later when I realized that the effort it takes to compensate for and deal with certain behaviors in the workplace, drained people to the extent that they did not want a repeat of this in their home and personal life. Viktor believed apparently, that it would in some ways compromise his credibility at work if he allowed people into his personal world at home, that he might lose face or no longer be accepted or respected in his role as leader. He therefore also allowed no contact between the office staff and his wife and children. He was an extremely intelligent man and seemingly successful so at the time I accepted that he probably had sensible reasons for his rigid boundaries.

After Viktor changed jobs and we were able to reconnect socially once again, I began to realize that he was a very different man at home to the one I had encountered at work. His wife, whom I had obviously known before I reported to him as manager, called me at one time and asked me for advice on how to deal with him as they were going through a divorce. It transpired that she herself was perplexed as to which of his behaviors were *learned* and inauthentic, and which ones were reflective of his true nature.

I spoke once with Viktor post-divorce, and came to the conclusion that so many of his behaviors were learnt (clip-on style) that he was completely alienated from his true self. He was struggling to find his personal identity which he had lost somewhere in his search for an acceptable professional identity.

Authenticity face-to-face

Reflecting on this experience, I sometimes wonder who the true person is behind the candidate I am interviewing for a position. It often appears that applicants are playing a role they have learned and taken on a persona which comes across as being phony or insincere. A persona and attributes which are certainly designed to impress. What is disconcerting is that I sense that the candidates in question seem quite comfortable in exhibiting what is deemed to be *acceptable* or *learned* behavior and seem oblivious to the fact that the interviewer sitting across, can very often sense that the façade is bogus. You just know intuitively when something doesn't sit right, you can't always put your finger on it, but you know.

Conducting an interview is simply so much easier when both the individuals experience one another's authenticity and openness. When this happens, it is entirely possible for there to be a more comfortable and non-threatening atmosphere where trust can be built between the parties.

I was asked once, whether I am able to see through the façade of candidates I interview and whether other see it too. I see it this way.

So often managers will say to me that they get the distinct feeling that something just isn't right. A gut feeling, if you will. I believe that this gut feeling emanates from the disconnectedness between the candidates' true self and their learned behavior. The experienced interviewer is able to discern that what the interviewer is verbalizing isn't altogether the true state of affairs behind the smokescreen.

The second part of my answer lies in the fact that experienced leaders and managers can sense phony behavior. They can tell when *learned behavior* is not integrated with the candidate's overall personality but *bolted on*. This learned behavior sticks out like a sore thumb in a behavior based interview when the candidate gives examples which have gaps and inconsistencies in them. The candidate may also struggle to expound on examples and try to fill the void by making comments which demonstrate an attempt at coming across as *appropriate* or valid when the substance of the example is decidedly on the lean side. The candidate may also include commentary which tries to put a positive spin on the rather bleak content as a patch-up measure.

Weinstein (2015) comments on such situations as follows: "Determining a person's character during a brief job interview or a series of interviews can be difficult. Meet this challenge by making the interview behaviorally focused. To spur applicants to reveal clues about their characters, ask them to talk about a time when they 'had to stand up to someone in authority'. Listen carefully to their answers; observe their body language and nonverbal cues with equal care."

The focus of the interviewees should really be on trying to relax and be themselves in order to allow the interviewer to experience and connect with their true self. The best environment is where there is open and honest reflection. When a candidate displays insincerity the gap between interviewer and interviewee widens.

Many people are able to *sell* themselves well, but I have found that these particular personality types are often the least self-aware. In addition, they don't appear to consider realistically how they might fit into the position, and what they really are able to bring to the table. People who tend towards these behaviors rarely admit to areas where they may fall short in order to be an asset in the particular position.

They are generally not open or honest about their areas of weakness. The fact-finding mission lies in the hands of the interviewer who has to unravel what the unspoken communication is saying about the person's suitability for the position.

This certainly can be a challenging task, but it is also a critical one. If we are unable to identify inauthentic candidates in our job interviews, we will be populating our organizations with inauthentic individuals!

Authenticity and its challenges

I stated earlier that total transparency is not being advocated as a precondition to authentic leadership. The challenge is to find a happy medium between distance and closeness, when to open your boundaries and when to close them, when you can disclose your thinking and feelings and when not, especially in unfamiliar situations. This balance can only be achieved if you know who you are and how you will react. In order for you to be able to judge how much you are willing to disclose you need to know and understand yourself well. Your self-knowledge needs to be intimate enough to enable you to judge what you should reveal about yourself and your thinking and feelings and will serve as the personal radar which guides you.

Walking around with your heart on your sleeve has never been a good idea in the business world and this is also true of your personal life. There may be times when you feel comfortable in sharing your emotions and feelings, and an opportunity may present itself where you feel it is the appropriate moment and the right person to be sharing your feelings with. However, others may experience this as overwhelming and inappropriate rather than you being authentic. Remember, that not all people are able to deal well with others' emotions or make sense of them, and many feels very uncomfortable with obvious displays of emotion and *oversharing*.

I would therefore caution anyone to maintain a balance between self-disclosure and discretion. This can be achieved by taking into account the context, the person on the other side, and how it will affect your relationship with them in future in your work environment.

Authenticity vs rationalization

Most of us have been exposed in some way or another to a greater knowledge of our weaknesses through feedback and reactions from colleagues and others close to us. This helps us to fill in the gaps so that we can understand and be aware of how our behavior affects them.

The difficulty we often encounter with feedback is, *rationalization*! We tend to rationalize because our brain quickly recognizes the discomfort we feel when our behavior or our thoughts are challenged or questioned. We attempt, through rationalizing, to give ourselves *permission* to behave in certain ways. Rationalizing is a means to protect our identity and save face, but it is a logical left-brain, response and does not align itself with the emotional, right-brain side. This response has its place and value, but we need to be aware that it exists, and that it is a risky business. It very often reinforces erroneous thoughts and behaviors.

Some people have the ability to rationalize explicitly in such an apparently logical way that nobody is able to disagree with their particular perspective. The down side of this is that it leaves the emotional side out and the encounter with that person feels *sanitized* rather than authentic. We may understand the person's logic but cannot connect emotionally with them. This emotional disconnectedness creates feelings of mistrust. We understand the *message* but not the *messenger* and so the message is heard but not assimilated and embraced.

Authenticity requires that the overt, verbal message being conveyed by someone, is in harmony or congruent with the non-verbal, emotional message that is conveyed. Be true to your *self*. When there is disconnect between the verbal and the non-verbal, authenticity will not be perceived nor transferred between two people. When this transference does not take place, people experience the interaction with their colleague, friend or boss, as being insincere. Often, they are unable to put their finger on why this interaction feels stiff or contrived and they are left with a feeling of awkwardness or uneasiness.

Final tune on authenticity

In this chapter I have tried to make you more aware of authenticity. I have highlighted what I regard as being the shortcomings of behavior modification techniques in overcoming leadership deficiencies. I have spent time talking about the role of self-disclosure and a willingness to be vulnerable in establishing authenticity. I have also highlighted the need for limited and judicious self-disclosure. I have honed in on the role of authenticity in recruitment and also discussed some of the challenges related to authenticity. Above all, I have tried to convey what it is to be authentic, what it means to be inauthentic and how these *states* profoundly impact on our effectiveness as leaders.

You and I can only be *attentive leaders* when we intimately know our own strengths and weaknesses and how they are expressed in our behavior towards others. Through establishing a healthy self-image, we are able to thoughtfully compensate for our weaknesses and manage them wisely.

This process, this getting to really, really know yourself, is why I have written this book to support you on that journey. As I have shared with you in regard to my own experience, it has the potential to be an exciting process of self-exploration for you. An exploration of – what you can *sell* about yourself, and what you should *tell* about yourself! This book is also designed to help you to compensate for and manage your weaknesses, or areas of development.

In the next chapter, "Defining the Journey" I lay a broad theoretical framework which I hope you can use to support you in your own journey towards becoming more authentic.

PART TWO

Attentive Leadership

Defining the journey

In part one of this book I developed the ground work and base for understanding what should be considered in developing a healthy self-image, which will assuredly increase your zest for becoming an authentic leader. In this second part of the book, I will develop a model that will help you to understand how your self-image is developed and sustained. I will be discussing what the building blocks are in developing your self-image, and with this shared understanding, we will be ready for part three of the book, where I will be taking you through a practical step by step process which you can implement to assist you in developing your self-image.

As you read this and the next part of the book, remember that the fundamental premise of this book is that authentic leadership flows out of a healthy and well grasped insight into self-image. It is vital for you the reader, to understand and digest the importance of the role that self-image plays in authentic leadership. I will therefore endeavor in this chapter to help you to do so by developing a theoretical foundation for self-image and by delving deeper into the related aspects of self-awareness, self-evaluation, self-esteem and finally pull it all together in the concluding part of this chapter.

In the process of developing my own theory, I considered studies on developing a healthy self-image, going back a couple of decades in order to form a picture of what these studies had defined and what the outcomes had been. I have found some of these studies as well as some of the statements they make, to be of particular relevance, and have included them in this book, hence the references to some fairly dated studies. I believe that the basic psychology of the nature of the individual has not changed much over the years – rather, it is the environment in which it exists which has altered considerably. Therefore, the same psychology has to be applied in a completely different setting, and that is our primary challenge.

Understanding the "self"

We are all familiar with the statement

> "Be true to yourself."

Have you considered though that in effect this creates a conundrum, because as Herminia asks, (Ibarra, 2015),

> "Which self?"

It is important to recognize that we all have many selves or dimensions to our inner person. Which self is likely to manifest will depend on the different roles that we play in life at any particular moment. This is why it is vital that we first define the concept of self-image and agree on what we mean by it.

The self-image consists of multiple dimensions, which interface with the true self. For the purpose of meeting on common ground, we first need to understand the interfacing between these different dimensions as well as what influence we have in establishing or changing this self-image construct.

I found a number of definitions of self-image in theoretical journals, books and articles, and realized that terminology pertaining to self-image is used interchangeably and frequently synonymously as well as indiscriminately. This tends to muddy the waters and cloud one's understanding of self-image. To ensure that you and I are on an equal footing and to cement your understanding of what I am referring to and how we can assimilate and digest the theory and practice of this book, I have defined self-image as maintaining the balance between the self-awareness (how you see yourself) and the self-evaluation (how others see you) to sustain a positive self-esteem.

Self-image is:

self-awareness x self-evaluation = self-esteem

In essence, what I am purporting is that self-image is developed from and upon a comprehensive construct. In concrete terms, self-image is the result of keeping your self-esteem intact; this means that self-esteem is created through a process, which starts with a high level of self-awareness combined with an equally high level of exercising self-evaluation – finding out whether your self-awareness is reality based and paralleled by the perceptions of significant others. The sum of all of these parts constitutes your self-image.

In terms of how I have defined self-image, this construct is certainly not easy to inaugurate or modify, because self-esteem can be volatile and change from one situation to another. Allow me to illustrate.

Let us take situations where you perhaps lack self-awareness in knowing what your competencies or skills are and how you evaluate these competencies or skills relative to the situation you face. For example, you may be unaware of your competence in making presentations (self-awareness). Or you may have some awareness of your general competency in making presentations, but be unsure of how well it will stand up to making a presentation to the board of directors (self-evaluation relative to a situation). Or worse still, you may be both unaware and unable to evaluate your presentation skills relative to a situation. In each of these scenarios you will experience uncertainty and are likely to find your self-esteem teetering on a slippery slope. It is very hard to imagine how you can experience a sense of self-confidence and self-worth in any of these settings.

On the other hand, your self-esteem may be very stable when your self-awareness radar is healthy, because you know what your competencies are, you are familiar with or can foresee consequences or results of how your competencies and skills may be applied in a specific situation or task. Self-awareness and the ability to self–evaluate removes uncertainty and boosts your self-esteem. If you are aware that you have good presentation skills, and in your estimation that they are at a level where you can present competently to the board of directors, then your self-esteem will be enriched.

I have worked with so many managers in all levels of business, who have developed competencies in their specific field of expertise, perhaps in their studies, or in a functional area, like finance or sales and who exhibit excellent self-awareness in this regard. However, when they move into a different role, e.g. that of a General Manager, they continue to trust this self-awareness pertinent to their field of expertise, but fail to evaluate the applicability and implementation of said competencies in the new position. We can imagine then, that the competencies and skills they already possess, are not necessarily relevant to what is now required of them as managers. This unknown and unchartered territory and absence of relative skills or competencies is difficult to navigate and the new manager's self-esteem experiences a derailing knock after the first failure or setback! There is a distinct disconnect between the individual's awareness and appraisal of his competencies relative to the situation, and what the situation actually requires which I am sure you will agree, can be quite a shock to the system and send this individual into an emotional tailspin.

This sense of failure may be prevented I believe, by the simple but necessary act of initiating realistic self-evaluation. This would help them enormously to understand what the limitations and barriers are in trying to apply their previously acquired competencies to a new and unfamiliar situation which calls for a completely different set of skills. The end result could potentially have been that their self-esteem would remain unscathed and not suffered a blow during this process of change. It would also have helped to keep them authentic and experiencing security in the new role.

Let us look at how this could play out in practice.

> Kate is a chartered accountant, working in a specialist role for a large firm of auditors. Over the years she has impressed her peers and superiors with her auditing skills. She is cognizant of her technical auditing skills (self-awareness), and also evaluates herself as being highly competent in applying these skills in her specialist role (self-evaluation). This self-awareness and self-appraisal has led to feelings of healthy self-esteem and a positive self-image in relation to her working self.
>
> Kate has recently been promoted into a managerial role, where one of the most important aspects of this role, is the ability to

lead and motivate people. From a self-image perspective, Kate is completely unprepared for this, because her self-image is tied up in her competence as an auditor. She has very little awareness of her people management skills, and is also not able to evaluate whether her skills set makes her equal to the leadership challenges of the role. This creates great uncertainty. In addition, trading on her auditing skills in dealing with people management challenges is not working, and the net effect of all of this is that she veers from a positive to a negative self-esteem in a work setting. How she responds to this challenge is critical. Does she go on a behavior modification course where she learns *clip-on* people management skills, or does she rather choose to be authentic and be open about her challenges with the people at work?

Does this mean that we should only accept or move into new roles which are safe and for which we already have a well-developed repertoire of competencies and skills? Most certainly not! Doing so will probably guarantee a degree of ease and success in the short term, which impedes personal growth. However, a vital component for success in new assignments or roles, is that we practice self-awareness and that we properly evaluate all relevant elements within the situation. This helps us to define a picture which shows precisely what our strengths and shortcomings are.

Once we have made this realistic evaluation and appraisal, we can develop a roadmap whereby we can compensate for the areas in which we lack knowledge or experience. We can do this by allowing room for the others in our team or environment, who possess those competencies we lack, to manage those tasks or assignments we are challenged with, in order to accomplish the desired end goal.

Before turning our attention in more detail to self-awareness and self-evaluation, I would like to touch on some of the hallmarks of a robust self-image and will briefly explain its link to authenticity.

Building a healthy self-image

Some of you are leaders who have proven that you can effectively cope with change. You are able to shift gears comfortably and make decisions and act upon them without necessarily having the whole picture in front of you. You do not become overly upset when things are up in the air, and don't have to complete every project or task before moving on to a new challenge. You are able to handle risk and uncertainty comfortably. You represent the transformational leaders in the world, and more especially so when you also exhibit other behaviors relating to connecting well with all kinds of people across hierarchies, up, down, and sideways, inside and outside of your sphere of influence. You build appropriate rapport, resulting in constructive and effective relationships and you know how to use diplomacy and tact to best advantage. You are usually able to defuse even high-tension situations comfortably. You are found to be a joy to work with and you are normally very successful as leaders.

This full package, dressed for success, engenders in others a sense of trust in your authenticity. Your employees and colleagues sense your solidity in your word and deed. They observe in your speech and communication, as well as your actions, that you are sturdy and robust within yourself. Your authenticity thus provides them with a secure basis for placing their trust and faith in you as their manager as you manifest as a well-integrated person who clearly possesses a healthy, realistic knowledge of self.

At this point, a healthy level of authenticity has been attained. Authenticity, I believe, means that others are able to experience you in your fullness as a complete person. By this I mean that even though your strengths may be obvious to others, they are also allowed a window into where they are able to observe and accept that you, like everyone else, also need to develop in those areas where you are weaker and may lack. Once this status quo has been achieved, you make it easier for others to build an open, honest relationship with your authentic self, because they are able to perceive and therefore connect with the real you.

I previously alluded to the fact that authenticity is the only characteristic which keeps you and me intact and which allows us to deal with and execute safe passage through all the uncertainties and changes we face in this rapidly changing environment. I would also like to reiterate that the only solid reference point in facing the future unknowns, should be that which is found within you. This reference point should be securely built on authentic self-knowledge. That is what will guide you in evaluating and re-evaluating yourself throughout the flux and fluidity of the changing phases of life and work.

In summary, in order for you and me to get to such a place of authenticity, it is important to build a healthy self-image on which you can depend and ultimately enjoy the benefits of having a balanced self-esteem throughout your life's journey.

As I have explained earlier, self-image is built through self-awareness and self-evaluation (appraisal by others). Let us explore these concepts and processes in more detail now.

Self-awareness

Self-awareness can be attained through numerous processes, and I agree with Pico (2015) who says, "It is a journey, one that takes time, courage, commitment, and patience." Pico suggests four ways of getting to know yourself better; coaching, psychotherapy, meditation and personality assessments.

Coaching and psychotherapy

Kets de Vries (2007) wrote in his article "Putting leaders on the couch",

> "Instead of just trying to examine and resolve pathological behavior, his aim is to make leadership a little more effective,

maybe more humane, (so that) it might have a positive effect on the organization."

I interpreted Kets de Vries's words as meaning that more than just coaching is necessary to bring some leaders on the right path of getting to know themselves – possibly even in the arena of psychotherapy, which is a deeper and sometime necessary route for increasing self-awareness, aimed at developing successful leadership qualities. This denotes a long-term reflection on who the person is and what effect their behavior has on the people around them.

Few leaders will acknowledge that they need psychotherapy and therefore coaching is more widely used to help increase self-awareness. During these coaching sessions, reflections are done on:

> The outside world or environment in which you find yourself
>
> Your own sensed behavior and feelings
>
> Your realm of thought
>
> Your vision, attention and intention

It is by reflecting and unpacking these aspects with a coach, that you will be better equipped to attain a higher degree of self-awareness and engagement with the specifics of any relevant situation.

Meditation

Tjan (2015) wrote in the Harvard Business Review:

> "... meditation is the practice of improving your moment-by-moment awareness. Most forms of meditation begin with focusing on, and appreciating the simplicity of, inhaling and exhaling. But these don't need to be formal or ritualistic, greater clarity can also come from regular moments of pause and reflection."

He refers to his personal experience, whereby he tries to gain greater awareness by simply finding a few seconds to focus on his breathing (often before sleep). During these meditations, he also asks himself a set of questions, among them:

> "What am I trying to achieve?
>
> What am I doing that is working?
>
> What am I doing that is slowing me down?
>
> What can I do to change?"

Note that the most frequent form of *meditation* Tjan practices, emerges through the executing of seemingly mundane tasks that surprisingly inspire a degree of therapeutic serenity, e.g. simple tasks such as washing dishes, working in his garden, and waiting for his son to be dismissed from his drawing class (Tjan, 2015). This, as I know many can affirm, is a simple, but highly effective and achievable method of meditation which is available to all of us.

Daily practices in mindfulness lead to great personal awareness.

Personality assessments

A number of leadership training and development modules use psychometrics to help the participants acquire a certain level of self-awareness, as a prelude to the process of reflection. A part of the training may then be devoted to reflecting on the results of the psychometric assessments, during the actual course. At a later stage, upon completion of the course, coaching may be made available to the participants so that they are able to more fully understand and make sense of what the psychometrics are revealing about them. This is certainly a very helpful tool in bringing leaders to an enhanced and more complete level of self-awareness and I would encourage any leader to make use of what this type of process can offer in order to increase self-awareness.

The report back to the participant (based on the results of the questionnaire) will be presented in a structured session (often by means of a full-round (360°) feedback). This is designed to help them to take the first steps in the right direction. If the participants knows themselves well, and possesses a high level of self-awareness, there should be no surprises or need for protracted discussions in terms of the results shared during feedback other than the assessor having to possibly de-mystify some of the language jargon used in the reports.

I would, however, prefer to amend *personality* assessments to *behavioral* assessments. Personality is a very broad concept and also something that is fairly unalterable or inflexible. That is not to say that we should ignore the dimension of personality as we still need to be self-aware in this aspect. What I mean, is that we should be more aware, of behaviors which our personality initiates and exhibits. Your behavior is what others observe and experience and that is what they react to. It is immensely important therefore to not only be aware of your behavior but also the resultant influence and effect it has on others and on how it is perceived by the observer. If you remain open to feedback from others on your behaviors this will also help you to understand your personality better.

Possessing such insights is a good and valuable starting point, but it will not suffice to merely have a general awareness of how you could, would, or might behave in light of how you previously behaved. Let's unpack this. A prediction of your potential behavior cannot unequivocally be relied on nor *anchored* by an assumption that how you previously responded in a very different dynamic, is how the untested future predicament will play out. In short, the hypothetical "what it could be and what I desire it to be" doesn't organically manifest into an actual real-time repeat in future unknowns. You may attempt to *plug in* to an envisaged behavioral reaction by using as your reference point something you have historically experienced. That is not unnatural, but please remember that there may be a significant gap between the historical frame of reference, and the reality you find yourself in. So, just as past behavior is a good predictor of future behavior this does not necessarily apply to new sets of circumstances.

What is the benefit of these awareness-exercises you might ask – and I have been asked this by a number of leaders who believe they are fully aware of who they are and what effect they have on others.

The question you and I need to constantly probe within ourselves, regarding our behavior is, "Is this behavior appropriate from my perspective as well as that of *others' perspectives?*"

To illustrate: There are so many instances when leaders show poor judgement in terms of appropriate behavior. Examples of this are the behaviors of leaders like Elon Musk from Tesla and Space X, Steve Jobs from Apple and Jeff Bezos from Amazon.

Schwartz (2015) wrote in The New York Times,

> "The three leaders are arguably the most extraordinary business visionaries of our times. Each of them has introduced unique products that changed – or in Mr. Musk's case, have huge potential to change – the way we live.
>
> Plainly, I have bought in to what these guys are selling.
>
> What disheartens me is how little care and appreciation any of them give (or in Mr. Jobs's case, gave) to hard-working and loyal employees, and how unnecessarily cruel and demeaning they could be to the people who helped make their dreams come true.

In fairness, the leaders all have loyal defenders. At Apple, for example, Mr. Jobs's successors – including Tim Cook, the chief executive, and Jonathan Ive, the chief design officer – have argued that Mr. Jobs matured significantly as a leader in his final years. Mr. Musk and Mr. Bezos have senior leaders who have worked with them for many years. But even an admirer like Mr. Ive remained bewildered by the way Mr. Jobs treated people.

"He's a very sensitive guy," Mr. Ive told Mr. Isaacson shortly before Mr. Jobs died in 2011. "That's one of the things that makes his antisocial behavior, his rudeness, so unconscionable. I can understand why people who are thick-skinned and unfeeling can be rude, but not sensitive people."

Given the extraordinary success of these men, the obvious question is whether being relentlessly hard on people, and even cruel, may get them to perform better.

Like their biographers, I think the answer is no. Our research at the Energy Project has shown that the more employees feel their needs are being met at work – above all, for respect and appreciation – the better they perform."

Herminia states: "Especially in times of transition and uncertainty, thinking and introspection should follow experience – not vice versa" (Ibarra, 2015). I am of the opinion that it is not always possible for us to first experience a specific situation (because we cannot force or manufacture it), in order for us to be able to reflect or measure how we might behave and respond. I strongly advocate that we begin a process of understanding ourselves in anticipation of times of uncertainty and transition through these methods of self-awareness described earlier, *before* we come face to face with difficulties. In short; prepare yourself in advance, to experience challenges, and be mindful of how you intend to cope.

I cannot emphasize enough how important it is to reflect, whether through psychotherapy, coaching, meditation or behavioral assessments and get to know yourself as a reference point for future unknowns and unfamiliar territory.

Only when you and I know exactly which strengths we can depend on, and how we will need to compensate for our weaknesses, can we successfully cope as a leader and specifically with uncertainty. To reach this point, we need to be intensely self-aware and know how we react to our environment and challenges.

Self-evaluation

The German language differentiates between *Selbstbild* and *Fremdbild*. *Selbstbild* is self-knowledge or how I perceive myself. Self-knowledge is however, only valid if I have integrated it with the *Fremdbild* (how others perceive me) and in doing so, gain insight into any potential discrepancies between the two. Self-evaluation is therefore not purely self-inspection and coming to a conclusion of who I am or what I can do, but rather a contextual understanding of who I am or what I can do, as seen by myself and by others.

The Johari Window (see Bibliography) was created in 1955 by two American psychologists, Joseph Luft (1916 – 2014) and Harrington Ingham (1914 – 1995). They used the model to provide people with a clearer understanding of their relationship with self and others. It is used in corporate settings as an exploratory exercise. Charles Handy (1990/1999) calls this concept the Johari House with four rooms and visually represents it as follows:

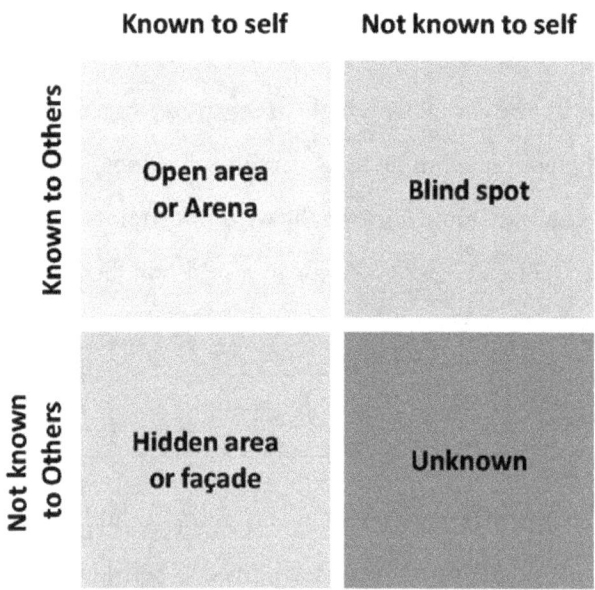

The Johari Window Model

The **open- or arena-room** is the quadrant that represents traits of ourselves that both we and our peers are aware of. **The blind spot-**

room represents information that we are not aware of, but others are; they can decide whether and how to inform us about these *blind spots*. These are the aspects that others see but we are not aware of. **The hidden- or façade-room** is our private space, and represents information about ourselves which our peers are unaware of and which we know but keep private. It is up to us as individuals to decide whether or not we want to disclose this information. **The unknown-room** is the most mysterious room in that the unconscious or subconscious part of us is seen by neither ourselves nor others. This room represents our behaviors or motives that will not be known or recognized by anyone. This may be, because they do not apply or because there is collective ignorance of the existence of these traits.

In essence, the Johari Window teaches that some things are known to ourselves – those areas represented by the open and hidden rooms, while some aspects of ourselves we are not aware of – the blind spot and unknown areas. What the model is designed to do, is to widen that *Open Area* or *Arena* so that a larger aspect of you as a person may become equally known by yourself and others. This is the ideal space in which authenticity can thrive and which allows for building and fostering relationships based on trust between people.

Remember, that it is only when your perspective of yourself overlaps and coincides with other's perspectives of you that you can truly say you have made an honest self-evaluation. Where these perspectives do not overlap, or *agree* with one another, you need to understand why the dissonance exists and what you can do to eliminate it. The broader the area of *overlap*, (open area or arena-room), the better you can be understood by others and be more transparent – this creates greater potential for you to be perceived as authentic. The goal of developing a balanced self-esteem, is more readily attained when you expand the open area, ingest feedback from others and establish your healthy self.

Feedback and authenticity

The matter of receiving feedback from others as part of the process of self-evaluation - of increasing the open area, the authentic space - does bring with it challenges and raises concerns that need to be dispelled.

You may for instance wonder whether you won't become a *fake* rather than *authentic* if you use feedback to change your behavior accordingly to suit the other person. You may be tempted to feel you are not being true to yourself. I certainly don't believe that to be the case. Feedback you receive should be reflected on honestly and subsequently integrated into your self-awareness (self-knowledge) and ideally should result in behavior changes for the good. Reflecting consciously on what is going on around you and in your personal space will only enhance the foundation building process for you to be your authentic self. Pope Francis put it succinctly when he said, "Choose trusted advisers who can help you make good decisions and aren't afraid to tell you when they think you're wrong." (Krames, 2014).

Fear of vulnerability is another challenge, as Stanford psychologist, Carol Dweck has shown, in a series of ingenious experiments on 'concern about how we will appear to others' and how it inhibits learning of new or unfamiliar tasks (Ibarra, 2015). We all want to perform well in a new situation, e.g. get the right strategy in place, execute at our best level, and deliver the results the organization cares about. But focusing exclusively on those things makes us afraid to take risks in the process of learning.

In order to alleviate this concern about how we will be perceived by others, we must embark on a systematic process of getting to know ourselves. In so doing we will be able to build a concrete foundation in understanding self. This can effectively counter the ways we inhibit ourselves in personal growth.

Creation and building of an authentic self should also not be confused with self-compassion, which forms part of the process, but does not address the full picture. Dr. Kristin Neff, who has spent a number of years on the subject "How to Build Self-Compassion", defines self–compassion as an adaptive way of relating to the self when considering personal inadequacies or difficult life circumstances. Whilst self-compassion is relevant, it is only one aspect that comprises the path of self-evaluation. Compassion has an element of emotion though, but I think it is more important to focus on a systematic process of self-evaluation, which involves reflecting with others in order to develop a realistic and healthy self-esteem. Only then can we truly achieve a well-balanced self-image which equips and empowers us to face the world of challenges and difficulties.

We also need to realize that human beings, with their inherently diverse self-images, do at times project their hang-ups and unattractive behaviors onto one another. When we personally experience this, we are provided with feedback which undermines rather than builds up. Such negative projection is often a compensation for low self-image. Leaders who project negatively tend to exude a strong message to those around them and convey the impression that "everyone else is wrong", or "just plain stupid", or that "they don't have a clue as to what they are talking about". They project an image in which they are the only ones who are right, possess wisdom and truth. Have you encountered such individuals? I think we all know someone like this and we should therefore also reflect on the accuracy of the feedback that someone like this is giving us. It is probably wise therefore to integrate feedback from several people into our open area, rather than that of a single individual.

Self-esteem

As I said in the beginning of the book, self-esteem is used in a very loose and non-defined way, so allow me to share a few salient thoughts on self-esteem offered by other authors before elaborating on my own tenets that I have already briefly touched on.

Habermacher, Ghadiri and Peters (2013) describe self-esteem as including self-worth and self-value (and is) ... also represented by an individual's confidence and ability to interact with the world. They make the statement that self-esteem is linked closely to well-being.

In the same research the authors refer to Epstein and Grawe who also propose a helpful model for understanding self-esteem. They link self-esteem to the fulfilment of five basic emotional needs:

> **S**elf-esteem
> **C**ontrol
> **O**rientation
> **A**ttachment
> **P**leasure

This means all human beings will in short, aim to increase (or protect) their emotional needs:

> "We would all like to feel a little more valued in the future (**s**elf-esteem), to have a little more freedom and control over our environment (**c**ontrol), to have little more understanding of the world and our environment (**o**rientation), to have warm and strong relationships (**a**ttachment) and finally to have an enjoyable and fulfilling life (**p**leasure)." (Habermacher, Ghadiri and Peters, 2013.)

They argue that it is essential for every human being to fulfil these five basic needs, whether they do so in the workplace or in their private lives.

McGraw describes self-esteem as a functional entity and describes the sensitivity of getting it in balance as follows:

> "Unfortunately, most people haven't got the foggiest idea of what self-esteem is all about, because they've been chasing after

other people's versions – that is, external sources of esteem – all their lives. For many, self-esteem or self-worth is too often measured as a function of what one accomplishes, accumulates, or extracts from the world in the form of titles, trophies, or acknowledgements." McGraw (2004).

He continues by making the statement;

> "The more your internally defined self-esteem is lacking, the more you are vulnerable to external influence. In short, if you aren't "squared away" within yourself, they can "get to you" from the outside. The world will pick on self-doubt like it is an open wound."

To encapsulate; although our self-esteem and by extension our well-being is not always honored by stakeholders in our environment, we will only do well by reflecting consciously on all the various dimensions in our lives which are enriching and add value to our self-worth. A workbook in the last chapter is available for this purpose. In this way, our self-esteem will be able to survive through situations where it is challenged or even assaulted.

This survival of our self-esteem has to be secured in many areas of our lives; sports, politics and in social circles, but of particular relevance, also in the business world. Leaders in business also want to fulfill or protect their emotional needs and the fulfillment or violation of these needs will influence how they think and how they operate in the workplace.

Fulfilling these emotional needs, is important in developing a balanced self-esteem. To be able to do this you will have to step back and reflect on who you are and how others perceive you – back to the model on self-awareness x self-evaluation = self-esteem.

It is only when your self-awareness is heightened and your self-evaluation together with feedback from others is on a firm foundation, that a more stable self-esteem can be established.

Through this process which functions in continuous circles, we are establishing a secure understanding of who we are and how we are apt to react in a specific situation. This reflection gives us a secure base to keep our self-esteem, which can be very fragile, intact. The more loops this process goes through, the better we get to know our behaviors and thinking in specific situations and the higher the level of authenticity we can reach. In this high level of awareness, we start to understand why we behave in the way we behave and what the effect is on others.

Recall too, that I noted earlier in this chapter that self-esteem can be volatile and change as awareness fluctuates from situation to situation. Another factor we considered is the amount of overlap between the *Selbstbild* and *Fremdbild* and that it should be maximized and brought into alignment as much as possible.

It is evident that your self-esteem can prove to be very stable under familiar and known situations - especially in situations in which you feel secure within your competency base or skill base.

Your self-esteem will also stand up to tests when your self-evaluation is realistic and accurate in how you and others perceive your actions, communication and behavior. That being said, when an unfamiliar situation arises, this perception and evaluation may need to be redefined and adjusted to fit the new situation.

Let me bring this closer to reality. A candidate whom I shall name Edward, once told me his story on accepting his first General Management-position. Edward knew that his strengths were in leadership and processes, but he did not feel comfortable with his communication style. He discussed this with his immediate superior and together they decided that it would be best for Edward to be assisted by an external *communication*-coach and that all his written and spoken communication would first be observed and assessed by the coach. Through the resultant self-evaluation and reflection with his superior, whose assessment of Edward's take on things corresponded with his, worked together on a strategy to improve Edward's style of communication, while applying the input and guidance from the coach.

After this candidate had operated for a while in the new position, he realized that his communication was not as poor as he had previously believed and that he felt he could manage and cope on his own. He again reflected on this issue with his superior and they decided that they would continue the development process on their own and release the external coach. What was the result? The candidate trusted his communication to be effective and therefore he could reevaluate his competency on his communication for the future.

This reflection and support, with honest feedback, created a secure environment for Edward to establish a good self-esteem concerning his communication capabilities and with time a healthy self-image.

Branden (1994) notes that a good self-esteem is sometimes confused with boasting or bragging or even arrogance, although he also makes the point that such traits may sometimes be as a result of a fragile rather than an overinflated self-esteem, and that these behaviors may be seen as compensations in the presence of an unhealthy self-esteem.

Tracy (2014) states that for a leader self-esteem is important, because the ideas and beliefs you have about yourself and the way you feel inside, will affect the way you are going to perform on the outside.

Is a healthy self-esteem dependent on your defining and over-thinking every single potential situation? No it is not. You will find, as your self-awareness improves, and where you are learning to trust yourself, that you can link different experiences and apply that self-knowledge to overcome barriers. This preparation can equip you to deal with even critical situations. The effort you invest in getting it right, should also be commensurate with the importance of the situation at hand.

Let's say you are presenting for the first time in front of the executive committee. You are fully aware that you possess presentation skills, knowledge of the subject and rhetoric. You have evaluated yourself as a good speaker, one who can hold the audience's attention. Your self-esteem, however, has not yet been subjected to any positive feedback from the actual experience because you have never before presented to the executive committee. If you do well, and you get positive feedback, you can add this positive experience to your repertoire and your self-image is given another pillar to stand on.

If you fail in this task, you may likely experience shame and embarrassment. You have a choice to react in two different ways. You can use the failure to add to your self-awareness library, become aware of and acknowledge the gaps, reflect on solutions with others in order to improve your competency, and in so doing, build on a balanced self-esteem. Or, you can hold onto the belief that you simply are not good enough to present to the executive committee. Opting for the latter course will most certainly injure your self-esteem. Making the right choice depends on your own will to honestly reflect on the situation and keep your self-esteem intact, while pursuing ways to improve inadequacies.

Brown (2010) noticed that one often believes that shame is only for others and that one should be protected from shame – this unfortunately is not possible, because as she states, "it actually tends to lurk in all of the familiar places, including appearance and body image, family, parenting, money and work, health, addictions, sex, aging and religion. To feel shame is to be human."

It follows that we have to ask ourselves how best we can deal with this shame as part of the *healing* process. How do we keep our self-esteem intact? Is there a way that I can explain or position my shame so that it does not destroy my self-esteem?

Herminia refers to Dan McAdams, a Northwestern psychology professor who has spent his career studying life stories, who describes identity as "the internalized and evolving story that results from a person's selective appropriation of past, present and future." McAdams says that you have to believe your story – but also embrace how it changes over time, according to what you need it to do. Try out new stories about yourself, and keep editing them, much as you would your résumé. Again, revising one's story is both an introspective and a social process."

This concept relates well to the way our self-esteem develops and establishes itself. The story which is our self-esteem goes through periods of change and sometimes needs modifying as it evolves. Over time in a healthy developing self-esteem, reflection and awareness becomes more complete and culminates in a higher level of gestalt.

The ideal is that reflecting on our *stories* becomes second nature. That we comfortably and easily self-reflect, and improve our habit of self-awareness and self-evaluation. That this process becomes less of a chore and more of an easy task. It is not dissimilar to the violinist playing an old favorite. He doesn't have to count every note, or try to play with technical perfection, because his musical memory is so well practiced. This is the positive balance we want to attain.

The foundation of a positive self-esteem allows us to explore wider and into more unknown and unfamiliar territories.

Self-image

Self-image can be seen to be built upon *pillars of experiences*. The more stable your pillars, the stronger your self-image will be despite being battered by uncertainty or challenging flux. It stands to reason, that too few pillars holding up your self-image may result in instability and run the risk of being knocked over easily so to speak. The number of pillars needed cannot be defined as this varies greatly from person to person and is relative to your specific circumstances.

What could these pillars comprise?

When I relocated to Switzerland, my reference points as a South African became utterly important. This identity-pillar was not that strong when I lived in South Africa, because I did not have to think about whether I fit in or not. It was an organic pillar, up until the point where my environment changed totally and I began to wonder to myself, "Where do I fit in this new environment?" I purchased my family genealogy, which has been well researched and documented. I traced and found my roots back in Europe. This process did not make me less of a South African, but I could answer a number of questions about myself and my origins, which the native Europeans could relate to and which opened doors for deeper relationships. I never realized how important is was for me to *belong* and this repositioning of myself in the international environment made the change-over much smoother.

When your pillars topple, the process has to start again with self-awareness being the first point of reference, the next step is to self-evaluate, and then make the right choices (as explained in my executive committee presentation-account), in order to repair your injured self-esteem, and so once again re-build your self-image.

This process of rebuilding takes place organically in that moment when you ask for feedback and reflect on your behavior, and then integrate this information with what your realistic self-knowledge tells you.

A number of leaders ask for feedback, but fail to integrate it into their own reflection on their self-awareness. They remain stuck on their own point of view and continue to exhibit the same negative behaviors in the face of feedback which is designed to give them a different but helpful perspective. In order for them to really listen and try to understand why the contrasting perception is relevant they need to be open to receive such feedback as a positive and not a negative. This truly is vital as a base for successful change and the growth process.

In my experience leaders who have learnt to automate this response are able to sustain a healthy self-image much more effectively than those who are not capable of switching on auto-pilot or quick reflection in this process.

You will find that employing a system of automation creates a sense of authenticity, because it is firmly based on dealing with reality. Why do I say this? Because using this method helps you, the leader to connect the dots in the reality of your self-awareness. You will learn to evaluate it quickly and re-establish your self-esteem. What do I mean by this? Simply that you as a leader will recompose yourself much more effectively through a quick reflective process. Engaging with the person who is giving the feedback will be helpful – especially by asking direct questions for the sake of clarity. Perhaps asking, "Allow me to understand what you really mean by what you just said – it is important to me if you want me to change this behavior."

"Authenticity is about a collection of choices that we have to make every day. It's about 'the choice to show up and be real" which is how Brené Brown (2010) describes the essence in cultivating this automation.

Is it easy to learn this method and how do we learn to automate this process within ourselves? In the next chapter, I shall explain the different aspects pertaining to self-image that we need to be aware of, but also need to evaluate with others in order to establish self-esteem grounded in reality. Once we have worked through all the relative aspects, pillars, a gestalt of your self-image can be achieved and established. The meaning of the German word gestalt is "a unified or meaningful whole". It stands to reason that when wholeness is attained a healthy self-image is sustainable.

Enjoy the process!

PART THREE

Attentive Leadership

Your journey

In this part of the book, we look at how you are able to develop a healthy self-image. This process is described in a theoretical model, with some tools in the Workbook. However, in order for you to benefit from the process, you will have to involve others whom you trust and whose opinions you value.

You may want to engage with a coach in order to thoroughly work through the reflection list. The assistance of a coach will prove to be an asset enabling you to work your way from where you are presently in your development to where you would like to be in your journey. You will find much to contemplate when you open the door of self-reflection and guidance in this process which will be of invaluable benefit to you.

Remember that this journey is a life-long one and doesn't end once you have worked through all the lists, but it is my sincere hope that the process will teach and equip you in how to deal with future reflections.

Take control of your own destiny

> "If people believe they have no power to produce results, they will not attempt to make things happen." (Bandura 1997)

Reflecting on this statement I think we can divide people in two categories. Those saying "I am what I am, because of my background" and those saying "I am what I am, in spite of my background."

McGraw (2004) refers to this as *locus of control*. He describes locus of control as the source or foundation of our power or ownership for the situations that arise in our lives. He states:

> "Generally speaking, people's locus of control is either external or internal."

And,

> "How people perceive their own locus of control determines, to a great extent, how they interpret and respond to events.

If your locus of control is external you operate from the mindset, "whatever happens, good or bad, is fate and I take no ownership or responsibility for it."

If your locus of control is internal, you operate from a self-image which expresses "anything good or bad that happens with me, I can decide how to act or re-act on it" (McGraw, 2004).

Dweck (2014), in her book "Mindset", says that this key psychological concept is the difference between some-one with a *fixed mindset* and some-one with a *growth mindset*. Someone with a fixed mindset has an external locus of control. Things are as they are and there is nothing I can do about it. Someone with a growth mindset has an internal locus of control, believing that situations are not set in concrete and that the power to change or influence them lies within.

Your mindset is not inherited nor is it hard wired, and Stacy (2014) agrees, "nature is neutral", so therefore it is what you make of situations that matters and will influence you. Each of us as individuals has the control and influence over how we will operate and function in life. Granted this will be shaped by the influences we have been subjected to in our lives and how they affect our behavior in the present, but the power to choose how we deal with situations still resides within us.

If you want to develop your self-image, you will need to align yourself with the "I am what I am in spite of my background" or *growth mindset*. Why is this? You need to want to develop and believe that you can grow in spite of setbacks or bad experiences. If you belong in the "I am what I am, because of my background" category you will be surrendering control to your past experiences. Before you can begin working on your self-image you will first need to shift your mindset from external to internal and believe that you can wield influence within your various spheres of life.

Snow (2014) states: "Making mistakes is part of learning, but human nature negates some of its positive results. The *attribution theory* holds that people make excuses for their mistakes but accept success as their due for their efforts and talent. Offering most people feedback, then, is a waste of time."

I do not entirely agree with this statement because I have found that people who make excuses for their mistakes are often those with fragile self-images and who have a real struggle in coping with failure. As leaders or managers, we should endeavor to support people who are too fragile to face mistakes and learn from them so that they are able to build a stronger self-image. They should be helped to make peace with the fact that making mistakes will always form an integral part of life, but that the end-goal is for them to learn from mistakes and thereby have a better understanding of themselves and be more integrated as individuals.

We are still wrestling with the question on how to develop a sustainable self-image. In this regard Bandura makes a clear (though theoretical) statement: "Self-concepts are measured by having people rate how well descriptive statements of different attributes apply to themselves. Their role in personal functioning is tested by correlating the composite self-concepts, or disparities between actual and ideal selves, with various indices of adjustment, attitudes, and behavior."

I believe that this complex process should be supported by coaching over a period of time. Change is not easy and we have to first gain the insight necessary to assist us in this process. Once we have insight, we can reflect on past and potential consequences related to our attitude and behavior and only then can we begin taking small steps in a direction of acceptance and growth. Bandura (1997) describes it in the following way, "… the self-concept contributes to an understanding of people's attitudes towards themselves and how these attitudes may affect their general outlook on life."

The process of developing a sustainable self-image begins by addressing the *self* in all aspects of life be it work-life, family-life, sex-life, relationships, leisure time etc. A thorough 360° understanding of your self-esteem in all these different areas of your life is necessary. Why is this so important? Because self-esteem is influenced by all the above sectors of life – they do not affect us in isolation and our brains integrate various experiences and feelings in these life areas into a composite whole. To illustrate, having an overall positive experience as a parent can quite easily *spill over* into how we deal with a leadership challenge for instance. And vice versa.

Does this mean that you and I are poorly adjusted individuals if we don't have positive images or feelings around all the various aspects which constitute our self-image? Unquestionably not. We do however, all need *anchor points* which stabilize us in times of doubt and turbulent weather. A stable *relationship anchor point* can for instance help to anchor us in other areas of our lives. These anchor points play a key role in making life worth living. We all possess them one way or the other, but we may need to work on defining them more clearly for ourselves as well and expand them. If our anchor points are not clearly defined we may find that in times of duress, we fall prey to being locked in a cycle of negative thinking and belief.

To illustrate: Suppose that you made a mistake which caused disruption in your work situation or even resulted in financial loss for the company. There will be enquiries and discussions around where you went wrong and these can very easily erode your belief in self and perhaps even your capabilities

Having said that, if you are able to draw on one or more of your *anchors*, where you bring into perspective a particular situation/s where you successfully and effectively executed your responsibilities in the workplace, it will go a long way towards helping you to discern and implement a positive take on the negative outcome in question. It needn't be doom and gloom and disequilibrium and one incident should not be allowed to handicap your development as far as self-esteem goes.

Edith Cooper, the Global Head of Human Capital Management at Goldman Sachs states:

> "You're not going to be great at everything every single day. Be clear about your priorities – to yourself and those close to you – and know that some days you'll be the hero at work and some days you'll be the hero at home. And that's OK." (Cooper, 2016)

In other words, sometimes being the hero at work on a particular day will help to anchor you when you are having a bad day at home.

Bandura (1997) makes an important point when he says that

> "people vary in the extent to which they derive a sense of self-worth from their work, their family, their community and social life, and their recreational pursuits. For example, some students may take pride in their academic accomplishments but devalue themselves in their social facility. Hard-driving executives may value themselves highly in their occupational pursuits but devalue themselves as parents. Domain-linked measures of self-worth reveal the patterning of human self-esteem and the areas of vulnerability to self-disparagement."

These examples confirm my hypothesis; It is only those managers who are integrated within themselves, who are secure in their personality and possess ego-strength, who successfully cope with the complexities they face in our present world. It is due to the fact that their reference point – their anchor, their locus of control – resides within. This eliminates the need to try to compromise and re-adjust their behavior constantly in keeping with the situation at hand and what is required to manage it.

Of course, we have to be aware of what is required of us in varying situations. In trying to deal with new and unfamiliar situations or conditions that you have never before experienced, the only real security in dealing with these situations, is to know yourself. You can hardly fail when you are deeply aware of your own convictions, how you deal with relationships, your competencies, or in one word, your *self-knowledge*. In a nutshell: it may sound clichéd but you have to trust yourself, by having a healthy self-image and relying on yourself to deal with the complexities of life!

I was reminded recently of how destabilizing it can be when one's self-image is fragile in some areas. I have worked in Human Resources for 30 years now and gained experiences in all the various fields within the function. In my present situation, we split the Human Resources department into two divisions – Talent Management (for which I am responsible), and Rewards (which Sarah, my colleague is responsible for). We both report to the Group CEO. I have been involved in recruitment since I entered this industry and part of my job profile involves handling negotiations with candidates, with respect to salary packages.

Recently we were in the process of recruiting a senior manager and the negotiations became fairly complex. The first thing my boss said to me was:

"Give the compensation negotiation to Sarah."

I was extremely annoyed, because I immediately interpreted this response as mistrust or a tweet of incompetence from my CEO. Nonetheless I handed the case over.

Upon reflecting on the situation afterwards I considered that perhaps my boss very possibly hadn't looked at it this way. He may quite simply have believed that my colleague possessed greater knowledge in this specific area, and might be able to resolve the negotiations more effectively, which I had to admit, rang true. Perhaps he even felt that I needn't be tied up with this negotiation in light of the fact that we had a specialist like Sarah in the house.

After this reflection, I immediately felt less aggrieved and I could still hold my head up. This is where my anchor point came into play. I had historically successfully executed thousands of salary negotiations at executive level. This incident made me realize just how sensitive I was to feedback that didn't boost my self-esteem. I fell into the trap of allowing my boss's decision to control my feelings and derail me. However, when I reflected and took back control by processing the situation more rationally and grabbing hold of an internal anchor point (my track record of success in handling salary negotiations), my self-esteem was restored.

I am convinced that sensitive people are disadvantaged in some ways, because they tend to *feel* and experience situations and people more intensely than someone who is less sensitive. This kind of sensitivity is usually the result of emotional struggles faced earlier in life. The more severe the emotional pain experienced in the early development years, the more sensitive the adult may become. Overly sensitive antennae and *survival mechanisms* are developed which serve as a means to self-protect throughout life.

True, there are plus sides to having a heightened sensitivity. One may for instance have greater empathy for other's struggles, but it also may handicap healthy development. The sensitive soul is constantly evaluating messages and feedback to test whether they are designed to harm or hurt. If our self-image is poor and renders healthy reflection difficult, we can easily become consumed and feel drained and run-down. We more easily succumb to doubts, and struggle to cope with malevolent influences in our world.

Sometimes, sadly, these sensitive souls who struggle to survive in a less than welcoming world, end up in a place where they succumb to resignation and where their underlying script tells them… "I am what I am, because of my background (experiences, feedback, interactions etc.)."

What then am I saying? Our lives can be controlled by the things that have happened to us, or indeed that are happening to us. These events and situations can determine who we are, how we feel, how we act. They can define us and control our self-esteem. We can resign ourselves to them, become stuck in them and *be their victims*.

Alternatively, we can look within ourselves and rely on our self-image, to take control of situations. The more we are open to developing our self-image and to cementing awareness of our numerous anchor points from the various positive spheres of our lives, the more secure and stable we will be in dealing with life and its challenges. When we operate from that inner space of self, we will also be more authentic in how we deal with others. I would like to express it in this sense – that the aim is - to be a self – directed leader leading from what is within you, rather than an adaptive leader who is continually reacting to external requests or stimuli. No doubt the real leadership challenge then is to become intimately acquainted with your inner self, and engage in a lifelong process of developing it.

In the workbook, you will have the opportunity to reflect on different spheres of your life and work out where you have great or lesser great anchor points and where your aspired identity lies, relatively to your consolidated identity in a particular sphere, e.g. you might have done well on all the elements of a sphere, but still have a different expectation about yourself in that sphere This gap might then be the essential reflective issue to work on. When you are well on your way to understand this aspired identity, it is inevitable that a secure anchor or reference point will be the outcome, with stability of the self as a by-product. You will find that working through each identity in the workbook, you will be able to cement more anchor points into your self-awareness.

It is important that you work through each identity in the workbook and do not just choose one that suites you. Some of the identities might be well developed and do not need any more attention and can serve as a strength to anchor on when the other identities are more vulnerable. We do not just live one identity at a time, but we are a whole person and carry all identities constantly with us. In this regard, PwC published a report in 2015 in which they state:

> "Bring your whole self to work; organizations actively invite the wider dimensions of their staff's lives into their business, explicitly recognizing that these will have a positive effect on their effectiveness. They will often fund activities that demonstrate the care they have for their employees as whole individuals, such as life coaching, team development and onsite childcare."

Developing your self-awareness

I have already discussed the importance of self-awareness in developing your self-image and in becoming an authentic leader. The importance of self-awareness is further highlighted in the PwC report, entitled: The Hidden Talent: Ten ways to identify and retain transformational leaders. This report also states:

> "Many of our current leaders have 'got to the top' through clear thinking and determination. We suggest that this will not be enough when facing today's wicked problems. In particular, there are five traits that may need to be compensated for:

1. Being over-confident in their opinions and open to decision making bias
2. Lacking empathy toward others, be it their organizations or greater society
3. Being rigid or inflexible in the way that they lead, as a by-product of their expertise
4. Denying the existence of uncertainty
5. Being ambivalent about the concept of personal growth . . .

Leaders who possess the ability to navigate successfully though this kind of complexity are different in some fundamental respects:

…. They don't need to be in the limelight, their ego enables them to take a step back which creates the opportunities for others to thrive."

These limiting traits are connected to and flow out of his self-image. Without becoming self–aware, leaders are doomed to fall victim to the counterproductive elements of these traits, to the detriment of the organizations they lead. For them to change, they will first have to become aware of where they stand in relation to these traits and which of these traits they need to compensate for. However, experience shows that very few leaders at the top of the corporate ladder seem to possess this awareness. This makes it a challenge to get them to voluntarily own the fact that their behaviors, thinking or feelings are the blockages for growth in the organization or are in part responsible for not allowing others to grow under their leadership. The cost of poor self-awareness is therefore indeed very high – the best people are leaving the leader to find a better environment to operate in.

The process of self-awareness, self-reflection and evaluation, with the help of coaches, colleagues, friends and others whom we trust should, I believe, start as early as possible in our career. It is a sure way to attain improved self-esteem and for a healthy self-image to be the inner gyroscope that leaders use to navigate a balanced path through complex leadership challenges – one that will bring out the best in people and organizations. Once leaders are on a path of success, which is not accomplished this way, but rather by using force, scare tactics or fighting to get their way, it becomes extremely challenging to convince such persons that reflection will create personal growth and greater leadership effectiveness. More often than not, it is only a crisis that will induce a reality check and motivation to change.

I developed the following schematic to facilitate the process of becoming self-aware, based on the model, "Total Life Space" of Jean Neumann from the Tavistock Institute of Human Relations (Neumann, 1999 and 2007):

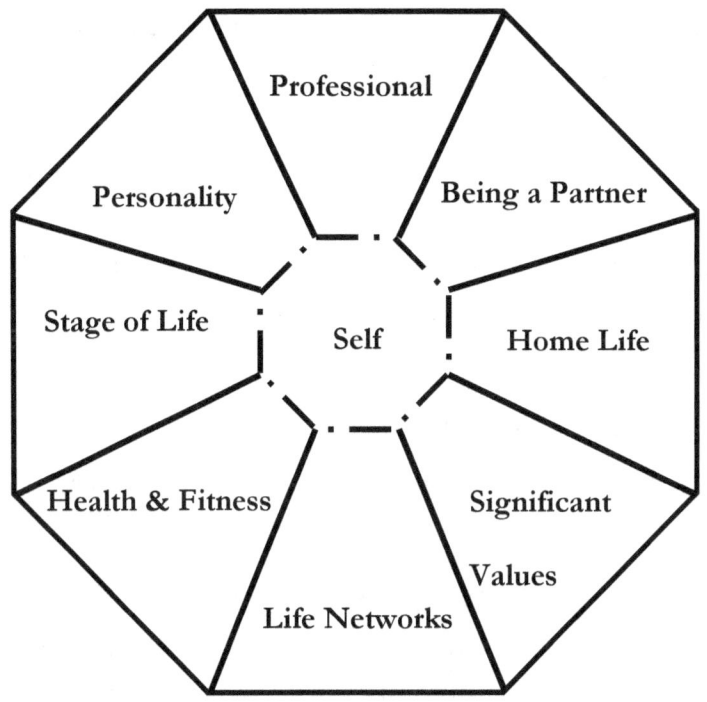

Each of these segments represents distinct identities that are built on your own perceptions, and establish a base for how you think about yourself. This self-reflection on your level of self-awareness, is more integrated than the results from an external assessment, whether by psychometric assessment or other means. (I have provided a questionnaire illuminating and clarifying the various identities which will help you to start on this reflection process - you will find it in the workbook at the end of this book).

I would like to discuss each of these identities and to provide you with a clearer understanding of each, I have used quotes at the end of each description. These quotes will help you to understand the essence of the identity and will give you more insight than simply reading through the lists of attributes associated with each identity would.

The **Professional** identity encompasses:

- ✓ Your occupational identity which pervades your current work, what you are doing and how you are doing it.
- ✓ The story of your professional life and how your vocation or profession has been developed.
- ✓ What enjoyable / fulfilling and not so enjoyable / fulfilling work means to you.
- ✓ You should reflect on the Place of Work (location); the characteristics of the location and related timelines you have been employed. Your roles, responsibilities and tasks form part of the full picture as well as the enactment of purpose or mission you have.
- ✓ The people you worked with or worked for forms part of this dimension.
- ✓ The degree of autonomy, variety, feedback, significance and visibility you enjoy at work.

Confucius once said: "Choose a job you love, and you will never have to work a day in your life."

"Your work is going to fill a large part of your life, and the only way to be truly satisfied is to do what you believe is great work. And the only way to do great work is to love what you do. If you haven't found it yet, keep looking. Don't settle. As with all matters of the heart, you'll know when you find it." - Steve Jobs.

"Pleasure in the job puts perfection in the work." - Aristotle.

The **Partner** identity constitutes:

- ✓ The intimate relationships you are involved in, whether it is as a marriage partner, life partner or in casual relationships. Is your sex life fulfilling and does it fulfill your needs?
- ✓ How you see yourself in such partnerships, the roles that are played and to what extent all parties' needs are met.
- ✓ The extent to which self-actualization is attained in these relationships.
- ✓ Here the understanding, insight and opinion of the other parties play a major role, of which an important factor is that there be consistency with both parties' espoused values and beliefs.

"Truth is, everybody is going to hurt you: you just gotta find the ones worth suffering for." - Bob Marley.

"We don't develop courage by being happy every day. We develop it by surviving difficult times and challenging adversity." - Barbara De Angelis.

"Truth is, I'll never know all there is to know about you just as you will never know all there is to know about me. Humans are by nature too complicated to be understood fully. So, we can choose either to approach our fellow human beings with suspicion or to approach them with an open mind, a dash of optimism and a great deal of candor." - Tom Hanks.

The **Home Life** identity constitutes:

- ✓ The physical space you live in, as well as roles, responsibilities, tasks and expectations towards and from others at home.
- ✓ The synergies of thinking at home or, indeed differences and how they play out in real life, reflect the home life reality.
- ✓ The community culture and enjoyment of satisfactory authority relationships complete this picture.

"A man travels the world over in search of what he needs and returns home to find it." - George A. Moore.

"He is happiest, be he king or peasant, who finds peace in his home." - Johann Wolfgang von Goethe.

"Home is where one starts from." - T. S. Eliot.

The **Personality** is described in:

- ✓ How much you have internalized good and bad attributes.
- ✓ What your accumulated experiences are.
- ✓ The complex meanings of life and the world you have built up over time.

- ✓ Here you also reflect on repeating patterns of behavior and interactions, possible psycho-pathology and neuroses.

"People change and forget to tell each other." - Lillian Hellman.

"Some days are just bad days, that's all. You have to experience sadness to know happiness, and I remind myself that not every day is going to be a good day, that's just the way it is!" - Dita Von Teese.

"You gain strength, courage, and confidence by every experience in which you really stop to look fear in the face. You are able to say to yourself, 'I lived through this horror. I can take the next thing that comes along.'" - Eleanor Roosevelt.

The **Stage of Life and Career** reflects strongly on:

- ✓ Your actual age and physical health.
- ✓ Economic implications you face, together with your ambitions and the time frame in which you want to achieve them all are in the arena of this identity.
- ✓ The knowledge base you gained to develop your career.
- ✓ The pace, quantity and demands of your work and the implications thereof in terms of your family, friendships and network exist in this identity.

"A dream doesn't become reality through magic; it takes sweat, determination and hard work." - Colin Powell.

Confucius noted: "The will to win, the desire to succeed, the urge to reach your full potential... these are the keys that will unlock the door to personal excellence."

"It's all about quality of life and finding a happy balance between work and friends and family." - Philip Green.

The **Significant Values** reflects on:

- ✓ Aspects of your background or upbringing, which define your overall identity (consciously or not).
- ✓ Recurring influences from people in earlier roles you had at a different phase of your life, plays a part here.
- ✓ Your extended family & friendship networks as well as hobbies & enjoyable pastimes and contributions can be reflected on.
- ✓ Your nationality, ethnicity, gender, sexual orientation and history plays an important role.
- ✓ Your views on people and how they change and develop is also relevant in this identity.
- ✓ Personal management philosophy and the events and people who shaped it. One's *choices* don't take place in a vacuum – most of them occur within a *social context* (Sunstein, 2015).
- ✓ Commitments to particular types of social change, social interests, passions, beliefs, religion and relationships all have relevance for reflection in this dimension.

"You must not lose faith in humanity. Humanity is an ocean; if a few drops of the ocean are dirty, the ocean does not become dirty." - Mahatma Gandhi.

"A people that values its privileges above its principles soon loses both." - Dwight D. Eisenhower.

"Our most basic common link is that we all inhabit this planet. We all breathe the same air. We all cherish our children's future. And we are all mortal." - John F. Kennedy.

The **Life Networks** refers to:

- ✓ Frameworks, methods & techniques which mostly influence you currently.
- ✓ Relationships with a mentor, whether current or internalized feature in this identity.
- ✓ Roles that are based on membership in other organizations, community involvement, volunteer opportunities, political party and social activism.
- ✓ Resource implications (cost, time, and logistics) of current training & development as well as first professional training & development should be reflected on in establishing the identity.

"Networking is an essential part of building wealth." - Armstrong Williams.

"Personal relationships are always the key to good business. You can buy networking; you can't buy friendships." - Lindsay Fox.

"Our minds influence the key activity of the brain, which then influences everything; perception, cognition, thoughts and feelings, personal relationships; they're all a projection of you." - Deepak Chopra.

The **Health and Fitness** identity reflects on:

- ✓ Your health or medical condition or unique / different ability.
- ✓ To what extent you are in charge (or not) of your own health and fitness – whether caused by conditions out of your control or your own doing.
- ✓ How you manage or give priority to your health; exercise, eat right and use alcohol.
- ✓ How you have attended to your mental health. If you experience a precarious state emotionally, to what extent do you seek out the help of a friend or resort to professional counseling.
- ✓ To what extent this condition has or still influences certain life or professional decisions, is important here.

"Calm mind brings inner strength and self-confidence, so that's very important for good health." - Dalai Lama.

"A healthy attitude is contagious but don't wait to catch it from others. Be a carrier." - Tom Stoppard.

"It is health that is real wealth and not pieces of gold and silver." - Mahatma Gandhi.

The model that I just have outlined provides the basis for the questionnaires in the workbook. The questionnaires are designed to be utilized as a practical tool that will help you to get started on your personal journey of self-awareness. You may recall from the Johari Window that you need to get feedback from others in order to develop a holistic and well-rounded awareness to effectively stabilize self-esteem. You can use the same questions outlined in the workbook when asking people for feedback.

There may be various permutations in boundaries between the segments of identities. In other words, the boundaries which exist between your *self* in the middle of the schematic and any other *identities*, will yield in response to how much you allow yourself to be influenced and involved in a specific identity. You may find yourself *too far in* the field of one identity and lose perspective of the other identities. You may delude yourself and not be truly honest in one identity, and conversely, you run the risk of being *too far out* of the identity and remain disengaged, or insufficiently invested to establish a healthy specific identity.

What I strongly advise, is that you return to your *self*, before attempting to make the transition between the *identities*. Before you move from one *identity* into another, take the time and space you require in order to attend to the needs of your *self* by self-reflecting on who you want to be and where you are now. *Identities* will pull and push you in ways that you may or may not be able to influence, but having said this, you are in control of your ability to return to your *self* in every situation. Make sure you are clear on the boundaries between identities and reflect on your thoughts and behaviors during the process.

Your journey has context

Leadership styles differ from country to country – what is seen to be acceptable in one country is not necessarily deemed to be acceptable behavior in our countries. I remember when I came to Switzerland I was perceived as being very aggressive in my leadership style – I felt that it was fine to debate and argue a point until you either have convinced the other parties or someone has come up with a better idea. This vigorous debating process however, was not favorably received in the Swiss industry. I had to learn very quickly how to lobby, influence and come to a mutual consensus in order to be acceptable by my colleagues' standards. In this sense, I believe that leadership and the authentic behaviors around leadership has context. It is not only the external context that defines leadership though, it is also how your behavior fits with who you are or who you want to be.

"A lot of leadership skills you learn at home. There is no leadership without a context."

This is what Professor of Leadership Development and Organizational Change, Manfred Kets de Vries, in a case study, wrote up after interviewing the parents of British entrepreneurial businessman Richard Branson, (Karabell, 2012).

Insead Professor of Organizational Behavior, Michael Jarrett gives a good example on the context of leadership.

> "Leadership success has to do with the way people think, the way they feel, the way they behave. This is more than charisma; this is our "default behavior". The way we see ourselves, the way we act…"

> "Three studies demonstrated that when individuals evaluated a member of a stereotyped group, they were less likely to evaluate that person negatively if their self-images had been bolstered through a self-affirmation procedure, and they were more likely to evaluate that person stereotypically if their self-images had been threatened by negative feedback. Moreover, among those individuals whose self-image had been threatened, derogating a stereotyped target mediated an increase in their self-esteem, so many manifestations of prejudice stem, in part, from the motivation to maintain a feeling of self-worth and self-integrity. That is, self-image threat may lead people to engage in prejudiced evaluations of others. These negative evaluations can, and often do, make people feel better about themselves. Prejudice, therefore, can be self-affirming. By using available stereotypes to justify and act on prejudices, individuals may be able to reclaim for

themselves a feeling of mastery and self-worth, often saving themselves from having to confront the real sources of self-image threat." (Fein & Spencer, 1997).

Having been born and raised in South Africa during the apartheid regime, a number of people asked me whether I had been oblivious to the wrongs of that system and why I did not act to better the circumstances of the many people who were badly affected by that regime. The apartheid context in which I was raised as a white South African presented itself to me as being normal. It was all I knew and was the only reference point from which I could construct my worldview.

The inconvenient truth is, that we suffer from *blindness* when we don't have another reference point to draw from, or when we have never experienced anything else. This makes it very difficult to evaluate our views or correct our behavior. In the same way, a social system, such as the apartheid regime or the extremism in religion (the war in Northern Ireland which ranged over years or the present ISIS are good examples) is able to create a *false* understanding and indeed acceptance of what is appropriate or acceptable. This incorrect understanding plays into people's self-image and may reinforce and maintain this erroneous picture, until such time as the individual is confronted with and exposed to different and healthier scenarios or alternatives. After such exposure and enlightenment, a person is challenged with new information and has to re-evaluate what his or her values are and whether they will be of benefit in order to maintain an authentic and integrated self.

A superficial or cursory scanning over the landscape of your life will not help you to grow. You need to deliberately and systematically reflect on the realities you have faced past, present, and may potentially face in the future. To reflect honestly on what is truly happening in the various phases of your life, what it is you think and feel about each situation, is of paramount importance. It is vital precisely because it helps you to create balance in your self-esteem. Let me explain – by recalling your experiences and reflect on the consequences it had and what the context of those consequences were, you can learn from the impact those outcomes had on your self-image.

Over my lifespan, I had to develop my own self-image, which came a long way. As a child, I had a very weak self-image and will do everything to please others. I would go out of my way to be accepted by others and seen as a great person. One aspect about myself I realized early was that through my sensitivity, I do become aware of my own emotions long before others can observe them. This was a great advantage, because I could rectify my thinking on these emotions before they build up and explode. This gave me a base for a very positive attitude and thinking pattern. At times, this positive attitude served me well and I could motivate others to stay on the same positive note, although the environment was challenging. This served as an anchor point throughout my life as well as my leadership positions.

Some of my colleagues who were more risk adverse would often criticize me for not contemplating all the dangers and problems facing us and that would force me to reflect even more on my natural optimism and what is really happening. I found that my employees who saw some opportunities rather than risks, had a better energy level and came up with better solutions than others who only sees risks and barriers.

This experience strengthened my self-image and therefore I could resign twice from very good positions in industry, because I was not willing to compromise my values. Through the positive attitude and energy, I had from previous experiences of how people react towards me, I could go into a labor market with confidence and do what I thought was right for me at that time – this is how I became an independent consultant, helping people to deal with uncertainty, today.

In your reflections, you **will** find that some aspects of your life story are negative. This is not necessarily a bad thing. I say this because you may not be entirely unhappy with that particular negative. In other words, you may have accepted and made peace with it and are therefore comfortable with it. So as long as the negative is ego syntonic (the behavior, value or feelings are in harmony with your needs as an individual) it can still work for you.

If I could illustrate: You might have run away from home when you were a teenager because you could not live with the people at home or accept their norms of life. Reflecting on it in later years, you might come to the conclusion that you became a more independent person, who could cope through storms in life without sinking, because you learned so much about yourself when you had to cope with life's challenges. You subsequently built up a wide repertoire of successful experiences and an awareness which bolstered a healthy self-esteem and self-image.

There is no general norm which applies equally from person to person. Your personal measure would be to know your own bottom line and therefore how comfortable and integrated you are around any particular negative which impacts you in life.

Having said this, there are certain rules during the process of reflection which are generally necessary and appropriate. Steve Harley (2014) refers to a number of them when he writes that "your gift is that one thing you do best with the least amount of effort. You have to identify your unique gift and make the most of it. Getting the most out of your gift and sharing it with the world will bring you happiness, vitality and a sense of fulfillment." He goes on to say: "Many people default to the status quo rather than confront their fears and self-doubt. Face your fears and they will be less daunting than you expect."

This would mean that you have to evaluate your self-awareness. It may easily happen that you trust your own awareness perhaps too much and live in your *own world* which may be somewhat removed from reality. This would be evidenced by the fact that others see you very differently to the way you see yourself. Reflect with trusted partners or coaches, so that your fears and doubts can be inspected more closely in order for you to make honest sense around your self-awareness.

If you are practicing self-awareness effectively, you will realize that you have some identities that are well-developed and others which need to be worked on. The challenge lies in addressing those identities which are not so well developed in a constructive way. However, if in some identities you have no control and are unable to change them, you may have to learn to make peace with them and live with that reality.

One of my favorite comments from Steve Harley (2014) and one with which I utterly agree is: "You can't succeed alone, everyone needs advice, motivation and inspiration." To this wisdom I would like to add the need to include a *reflection partner*, whether that is a coach, a mentor, a friend or an acquaintance. The fact is that everyone needs a confidante with whom to reflect; which will enable us to practice realistic and reliable self-evaluation habits.

Assessing your journey

Assessment and feedback are some of the most challenging aspects in this process of developing a stable and authentic self-image.

What we need, is to get real and unfiltered feedback on ourselves and our defined self-awareness. If the person giving you feedback is sensitive and afraid that the feedback might hurt you, the person might be tempted to filter the feedback and perhaps provide you with positively distorted and inaccurate messages about yourself. In contrast, where the person giving feedback is insensitive, the information might hurt you to such an extent that you either reject or rationalize it. This is why it is very important that feedback should be sought from candid and empathic individuals. In this process, you should adopt an attitude of openness and be prepared to receive feedback about yourself that is outside of your awareness. It follows that sometimes feedback will surprise you as it shines a light on your Johari Window blind spot, but this is exactly when you need remind to yourself of the gift that this feedback potentially holds for you and adjust your response accordingly.

As Karabell (2012) reminds us:

> "Simple self-assessment can be a delusional activity due to the desirability factor that makes for a distorted self-image. To receive feedback from others helps people to have a more accurate look at themselves – superiors, employees, friends, family members, whatever - to get things on the way." As the saying goes, "If one person tells you, you have ears like a donkey, ignore it, but if two people tell you so, get yourself a saddle."

There are different ways in which we can get honest and accurate feedback. A 360° feedback where the candidate's feedback source can be anonymous, can be a very helpful form of assessment and feedback. In one of the organizations I worked for, we for instance developed a 360 App. This app allowed anyone to request colleagues to provide them with feedback on a range of issues. To ensure validity and objectivity, a feedback report would only be generated once more than one person responded to a colleague's request for feedback. The app was also set up in such a way, that those providing feedback remained anonymous which as can be expected ensured that the feedback was candid and realistic.

Assessment and feedback can also take place with close *confidantes*, friends or colleagues with whom you have already established a basis for trust. Care should be taken though that this trust is two-way where the person giving you feedback feels that it is fine to be honest with you, and where you have sufficient trust in the person to accept the feedback as being valid and authentic.

In-depth awareness training is commonly used in most business school curriculums nowadays to facilitate the process of assessment and feedback. This can be an invaluable tool and managers often positively acknowledge the feedback given by coaches during such training. It has its limitations however, because feedback is given by an *outsider* who is not privy to the circumstances peculiar to said manager, as a result the impact may be less effective and because of its *once-off* nature, is not always a sustainable basis for growth. Rationalization by the candidate often ensues which effectively negates the feedback received, once the manager returns to *real life*.

The options and methodologies for assessment and feedback I have discussed so far all have their place. However, the most important competency we have to learn to use is that of on-going self-reflection and from there to develop a system that we can implement to address those issues that are illuminated by this self-reflection. It should be a continuous cycle. This is well illustrated by one of our managers, whom I shall call Martin.

Martin was a highly driven and ambitious person who was bent on reaching the top of the corporate ladder – his end goal was to be a CEO with full Profit & Lost-responsibility. His manager had some concerns about him and so Martin was sent to a training event where he was made aware of his behavior by means of a comprehensive battery of psychometric tests and a 360° feedback. The developmental areas that were highlighted in the assessment were that he had no interpersonal reflective capabilities and that he tended to project his own insecurities onto others. Combined with his eagerness and over-ambition to climb the career ladder, a real danger to derail his career was created. His manager had sent him on the training session precisely because he wanted to avert this seemingly inevitable outcome.

Martin returned from the training with an improved awareness and provided his 360° participants with a picture of what he believed he had to work on during the next six months, and he assured them that he would follow a program which would assist him in his endeavors. The gap in this potential development was that he wasn't given any direct follow-up evaluation or assessment in how he was shaping up at changing those negative behaviors which had been brought to his attention. Sadly, it wasn't long before he fell back into old patterns and behavior. He went back to being overly demanding, overly ambitious, blaming others and the system for the fact that he was being hindered from achieving his personal goals.

In terms of the goals he did achieve, Martin left a trail of casualties in his wake. So, despite the fact that his self-awareness was addressed in training, and that he was helped to reflect with the input of coaches, nothing positive or lasting had been achieved. What was missing from the *development program*, was that Martin had not been taught from the outset, to constantly reflect and evaluate feedback, intensify awareness, get real time feedback, reflect on it again and that this was an exercise that would need repetition for permanent positive results to be achieved. In a nutshell, he did not return to the proverbial drawing board to repeat the process I just described, which would have gone a long way towards his building a balanced self-esteem to carry him through the challenges he faced in his career.

A colleague outside of his team commented that Martin exhibited a very low self-image and that this factor fed into his need to prove himself and that he always "had to be right". The only way Martin would ever successfully address this, would be by engaging in on-going reflection.

I can only conclude, and I am sure you will agree from this example; that external pressure to participate in training programs will not in itself be an agent for change in anybody. If we don't make the connection that we are the tool in the toolbox, and that if our equipment is faulty, our leadership abilities will be compromised, we are heading for failure and disappointment. Our *equipment* and the tool, which is our *self* must translate into our behaving in authentic ways. In a recent workshop someone provided me with valuable feedback when he said "In previous workshops I have been given tools to be a good leader, but today I realized for the first time, that I am that tool." This makes it clear that leadership is not about learned behaviors or trying to act and react in a predefined manner. In truth, leadership is about being yourself, being authentic, so that you as the *tool* in the system, can be truly effective and robust in your leading of others.

The challenge is to teach people how to reflect constantly and in so doing develop a system, a way of thinking about yourself, to grow from and build on feedback. Reflection should be a regular habit and ideally become second nature. This prepares you for moving onto the next level of awareness. The sensitivity which arises from this programming is essential in going forward to establish a healthy self-esteem, which benefits self-image and ultimately results in you functioning as authentic leaders. To illustrate, the last CEO I reported to was a highly reflective person, who would invite a team and start reflecting with them on their activities and what the desired outcomes of these activities were. He would challenge those who were inclined to play the role of the victim and blame others for their shortcomings. He used the process of reflection with the team until he understood the results and consequences of their activities. From the insight he gained he would tailor his decisions on further actions and budgets. He was extremely aware of his behaviors, thinking and feelings and could talk about them at ease and with insight. Now *that*, is authentic leadership at its best!

The connection between assessment and awareness should be a constant feature as a vehicle through which you and I change the way we think about ourselves. This creates an ideal balance for healthy self-esteem.

The self-esteem journey (and potential de-railers)

> "Self-esteem is a subjective evaluation of how a person feels about himself - a composite measure of one's perception of competence and feelings of security and confidence and a recognition of one's strengths and weaknesses. A person's self-evaluation is determined by the degree to which his successes approach his expectations in those areas that are personally important. Either too few successes or too high expectations may result in a poor self-evaluation and low self-esteem." (Hill & Ritchie, 1977).

Over-simplification

Branden (1994) states clearly that in terms of dealing with self-esteem, we need to be aware of two dangers.

> "One is that of oversimplifying what healthy self-esteem requires, and thereby of catering to people's hunger for quick

fixes and effortless solutions. The other is that of surrendering to a kind of fatalism or determinism that assumes, in effect, that individuals 'either have good self-esteem or they haven't,' that everyone's destiny is set (forever?) by the first few years of life, and there's not much to be done about it (except perhaps years or decades of psychotherapy). Both views encourage passivity; both obstruct our vision of what is possible."

Lack of confidence

Self-esteem to Branden (1994) is

"Confidence in the efficacy of our mind, in our ability to think. By extension, it is confidence in our ability to learn, make appropriate choices and decisions, and manage change."

Over-protectiveness

If our aim is to fulfill our basic needs which talk into the anagram SCOAP (self-esteem, control, orientation, attachment and pleasure), we discussed in an earlier chapter (SCOAP – Habernacher, Ghadiri and Peters, 2013), we will be proactive in trying to uphold and satisfy these needs. To be able to fulfill these needs we have to be prepared to take on the challenge of creating a better self-esteem. Having said this, one has to note that some people try too hard to *protect* their self-esteem, instead of exploring new experiences or activities for personal growth, and therefore they end up stagnating instead of moving forward. I so often find leaders who seem incapable of self-reflection who are inclined to blame everyone else for what went wrong, and to absolve themselves in the process. In neglecting to own responsibility in regard to failures – they forget that they are the very leaders of the malfunctioning team and are thus even more accountable than the team as an entity.

Resistance to change

I have often experienced difficulty in trying to motivate and galvanize people who tend to confront comments and feedback with negativity. They habitually incline towards this negative path to the extent that others conclude that they are pessimists and give up trying to encourage and help them grow. This negative mindset ultimately creates more insecurity and weakens an already fragile self-image. It becomes very difficult and a real energy-drain to know where to begin to influence such people in a positive way.

Emotional/Physical fragility and exhaustion

When we are feeling tired or fragile emotionally we don't always think about the way we say things or behave. An example to illustrate might be the following: Tony and Anne's friends invite him over for dinner while she is away on a trip abroad. Anne telephones Tony to chat, and he mentions that he was invited for dinner to their mutual friends and that he is looking forward to a decent home-cooked meal again. Her knee-jerk reaction is "Why do they invite you when I am not home? What do they have against me?"

No, their friends aren't thinking in that tone at all. This incident could have been handled in a number of ways, if Anne had allowed herself a moment of reasonable reflection. Firstly, she might have responded – "Thank them from me for looking after you while I am away", and secondly "I would have loved to be there as well but we can make up for that when I get back." Anne might also have said "I am feeling unhappy about this, because I feel excluded and would have loved to be there too", or "I am feeling lonely being so far away from home and would have loved to be part of the get-together." The above proposed responses would have reflected a healthy self-image and reacting this way would not have compromised or hurt Anne's self-esteem, nor would it have created potential for conflict.

What is within your control?

The author and leadership guru Stephen Covey (Scott Belsky, 2010) encourages us to only focus on concerns that we have control over. He outlines the *circle of concerns* as being all of the issues that worry us – and then describes a smaller *circle of influence* (within the larger *circle of concerns*) which only contains things that we can actually control. His viewpoint, is that we should only expend our energy on issues that we can do something about. Focus only on problems that lie within your *circle of influence*.

Some people have a tendency to want to control and tackle every single problem that emerges. This is a very unhealthy dynamic. When we start obsessing over details and trying to fix everything which does not fit into our *circle of concerns*, we are heading for guaranteed burn-out, frustration and unnecessary stress.

Coping with negative feedback

It is good to remind ourselves that while we are on our journey there will be times when we are exposed to awareness and evaluations which are by nature very negative. This certainly does not mean that the outcome has to have negative impact or that the negatives be allowed to damage or create imbalance in our self-esteem. It is reasonable to deduct that there will also be times when we will receive wholesome and positive assessments and awareness and we must learn to draw on these in order to counter-balance unpleasant experiences.

What is important in light of the above is that we don't need to be flawless, angelic or god-like beings in order to possess a well-balanced self-esteem. We do however, need to be cognizant as to how various negative and positive dimensions impact on our behavior, decisions and how comfortably we deal with other people.

To quote Branden (1994):

> "The more solid our self-esteem, the better equipped we are to cope with troubles that arise in our personal lives or in our careers; the quicker we are to pick ourselves up after a fall; the more energy we have to begin anew."

2500 years ago, a great Chinese philosopher, Confucius, said: "Our greatest glory is not in never failing, but in rising every time we fail."

Self-esteem and active listening

Active listening and response is a way in which a leader improves interpersonal relationships in the workplace. To illustrate: One of your employees makes a proposal to you. You respond "Yes" to affirm, and then add "and…" before responding further. When you do this, instead of saying "Yes, but" … you are showing your openness for participation without fear (Leonard & Yorton, 2015). This confirms your interest and engagement with the speaker. Often, people think they are listening when they really are not. They are already busy formulating a response and so they miss exactly what is being said. Listening properly means *staying in the moment* without rushing the speaker or interpreting what is being said, and without forming your own response while the other person is still talking.

A good leader needs to be able to listen with intent in order to properly understand what is being said, and only then connect in response with the speaker. When you do this people will also appreciate and respect that you take them seriously and value their input.

Why is active listening so important? Branden (1994) affirms the importance between self-esteem and active listening, by saying:

> "The healthier our self-esteem, the more inclined we are to treat others with respect, benevolence, goodwill, and fairness –

since we do not tend to perceive them as a threat." He closes his argument with a very important statement: ". . . since self-respect is the foundation of respect for others."

Too much of a good thing?

Branden (1994) also asks whether it is possible to have too much self-esteem? He answers with this powerful statement:

> "No, it is not; no more than it is possible to have too much physical health or too powerful an immune system."

To conclude: self-esteem is a fluid and dynamic attribute, which is influenced by a number of variables. I fervently hold to the belief that if you are highly self-aware and have consistently exercised diligent reflection in terms of your self-evaluation, your self-esteem will be on solid ground and decidedly more stable. We should not, however, dismiss the variables which are inevitably going to have an influence on this process of building our self-esteem.

WORKBOOK

Reflective questions:

In the previous chapter I discussed eight areas or pillars of identity, namely

- Professional
- Being a partner
- Home Life
- Significant Values
- Life Networks
- Health and Fitness
- Stage of Life/Career
- Personality

In this Workbook, I provide you with questions relating to each pillar of identity. These questions are designed to lead you in the process of self-reflection within these different identities. Working through them will help you to become more self-aware with respect to your identity as a professional, a partner, in the context of your home life and so on.

Your response to the questions will provide you with the insight you need throughout the self-assessment and personal reflection exercises. The goal you want to keep in the forefront, is that of building your self-esteem in authentic mode. This is achieved by going step-by-step through all the pillars of identity. After you have worked through your self-awareness exercise, by filling out the questionnaire yourself first, you can revisit the same with a self-evaluation exercise, by reflecting your answers with a confidante.

Remember that each separate identity as outlined, should be considered on its own initially. Once you have gained a proper level of understanding as to how each identity correlates with your evaluation of self, you can broaden your application of how the identities connect with one another; how they are inter-related and inter-dependent.

Don't be discouraged if at first you struggle to connect all the dots – as you become more adept at maintaining a high level of self-awareness through self-evaluation and you feel more comfortable in relating to your *new, improved* self-esteem, you will be able to correlate how the various identities, whilst being separate, are still conjoined to make the whole of you. Be patient, do the exercises faithfully, and you will reap a bountiful harvest!

Keep in mind as you are working through this process that the *why* is a vital composite in this journey. The whole point of going the hard yards is so that you are able to gain a lucid and clear understanding of who you are, of what your *anchors* are, and what your development areas are. Again, keep asking yourself, "Why?" Our reasons will be unique to our own life journey, but at the heart, it is absolutely in order to achieve personal growth.

Once you have reflected on and answered all the questions in a particular identity pillar, take some time to reflect further on your answers, and then try to integrate them in the section

My…identity is….

Your next step should then be to define your aspirations relating to that particular identity and then complete the section

I would like my … identity to be . . .

I wish you every enjoyment in your quest to reflect on yourself and become more self-aware, evaluate that awareness and ultimately establish a stable self-esteem and cultivate a healthy and authentic self-image.

I have included some personal examples, where I believe it may assist you towards deeper reflection. These are of course, my own reflections and not a prescription for how yours should evolve, they are merely a guide to help you creatively. Make it your aim to make your own reflections as free as possible. In the beginning it might be more like a brainstorming session, but upon further reflection, the essence will become more apparent to you.

You can do it! And I mean that in the most sincere, authentic way! You can look forward confidently, to playing your instrument of choice with the freedom which practice affords, without sabotaging the rest of the players in the orchestra, nor indeed your own musicality! Gary Player, the famed world golfing champion once said – "The more I practice, the luckier I get!"

One last thing… don't forget to enjoy the journey!

IDENTITIES

Professional identity

My current job is . . .

My current job could be . . .

Work I dislike is . . .

Work that gives me energy is . . .

My place of work is . . .

My time spent at work is . . .

Staying at my place of work would be . . .

The purpose of my job is . . .

My responsibilities are . . .

My role in my job gives me . . .

The future in my job is . . .

My colleagues at work are . . .

My boss at work is . . .

In my job, I have autonomy to . . .

The variety in my job is . . .

The feedback I get on my job is . . .

The added value I create in my job is . . .

The recognition I get from doing my job is . . .

In my job, I am seen as . . .

My professional identity is . . .

e.g. My professional identity is that I know how to deal with uncertainty and ambiguity. I am aware of how change affects our work environment. I am capable of translating that knowledge into practice and know where I stand in terms of how I change.

I would like my professional identity to be . . .

e.g. I am foremost a psychologist and secondary to that an experienced Human Resources executive. I want to remain congruent.

Partner identity

My relationship with my partner is . . .

In this relationship, our values are . . .

Our intimate life is . . .

Our belief system is . . .

For me, our sex life is . . .

In my partnership, my role is . . .

In my partnership, my needs are . . .

In my partnership, I feel myself . . .

The needs of my partner are . . .

This partnership gives me . . .

My partner is . . .

To my partner, I am . . .

My partner identity is . . .

e.g. We share the same values, especially on religion. We can have open and honest conversations with each other and my wife understands me very well.

I would like my partner identity to be . . .

e.g. Just stay as you are and be with me for the rest of my life.

Home Life identity

My home is . . .

My responsibilities at home are . . .

At home, the expectations are . . .

(If applicable), the expectations I have as a parent are . . .

The people living with me at home are . . .

Our thinking is . . .

The synergies we have are . . .

Our differences are . . .

The culture at home is . . .

The relationships at home are . . .

My home life identity is . . .

e.g. I am seen as the head of the family and care financially for the family. I also enjoy wonderful relationships with my children.

I would like my home life identity to be . . .

e.g. I would appreciate it if my family would be more aware of my intention to provide for them, not only materialistically, but also emotionally.

Personality

My best attributes are . . .

My worst attributes are . . .

I experienced . . .

The meaning of my life is . . .

My world is . . .

I constantly behave . . .

My interactions with others are . . .

I am still working on myself in the area of . . .

The issues I still wish to resolve are . . .

The thing I am most proud of is . . .

The issues with myself I shall never be able to change are . . .

The behavior that gets me into trouble the most is . . .

My behavior most are appreciative of is . . .

My personality is . . .

e.g. I am action driven, with a high sensitivity towards the oppressed. I need acceptance from others and invest a high degree of trust in relationships.

I would like to have a personality that . . .

e.g. I would like to integrate the different dimensions of my personality more.

Stage of Life and Career

At my age, I am . . .

I assess my physical health as . . .

Economically I am . . .

My ambitions still are . . .

In the near future, I would like to . . .

Eventually I would like to . . .

The pace with which I build my career is . . .

The knowledge base for my career is . . .

At this moment in time, I am . . .

The pace at work is . . .

The demands at work are . . .

The influence my career has on my family is . . .

The influence my career has on my friendships is . . .

The networks I have created throughout my career are . . .

My career is . . .

My career is known for . . .

My stage of life and career is . . .

e.g. I am at an experienced stage in my life and am satisfied with my economic situation. I have reached the top of my career in industry and am less vulnerable to critical feedback.

I would like the stage of my life and career to be . . .

e.g. I need a new challenge which will stimulate me mentally and I have an eagerness to meet others with whom I can purposefully interact for the rest of my working life.

Significant Values

My upbringing created in me . . .

My background is . . .

The hero in my life is . . .

The *bad guy* in my life is . . .

The stabilizer in my life is . . .

My parents are . . .

My family is . . .

My friends are . . .

My hobbies are . . .

My pastimes are . . .

My subscriptions are . . .

My nationality creates in me a . . .

My ethnicity creates in me . . .

My gender creates in me . . .

My sexuality creates in me . . .

My sexual orientation creates in me . . .

My history is . . .

My view on how people develop is . . .

My personal management philosophy is . . .

I believe social change is . . .

My interests are . . .

My passions are . . .

I believe in . . .

Religion and I are . . .

My relationships are . . .

My significant values are . . .

e.g. *I uphold the value of fairness to all. I care for people and will jump in to help where-ever I see someone struggling.*

I would like my significant values to be . . .

e.g. *I am satisfied as to how my values developed over the years and I do get very positive feedback on my personal values.*

Life Networks

What influences me mostly is . . .

My mentor's / coach's influence on me was . . .

My mentor / coach still influences me in . . .

My organizational membership creates in me . . .

My community involvement creates in me . . .

My volunteering opportunities create in me . . .

My political activities create in me . . .

My social involvement creates in me . . .

My professional training creates in me . . .

My development creates in me . . .

My life networks are . . .

e.g. I am currently serving on the international Supervisory Assembly of a NGO and am board member of the same NGO in Switzerland. I am also an auditor of Business Schools and serve on an academic advisory team to a University. I enjoy the different activities and connections.

I would like my life networks to be . . .

e.g. I would like these networks to bring me in contact with people I might not meet on my every-day journey.

Health and Fitness

My health is . . .

My medical condition is . . .

My unique ability is . . .

My control over my health is . . .

My control over my fitness is . . .

My eating habits are . . .

My drinking habits are . . .

My exercise habits are . . .

My mental health is . . .

In practicing mental health, I . . .

When I am emotional I . . .

My decision making during emotional times, is built on . . .

My health & fitness identity is . . .

e.g. I try to eat to live and not live to eat (especially after 50). I do exercise regularly and keep myself fit – also to maintain my level of energy.

I would like my health & fitness identity to be . . .

e.g. I would like to enjoy the quality of life that I have now, while enjoying optimum physical health until my life comes to an end.

BIBLIOGRAPHY

Bachelder, Cheryl, 2015, Dare to Serve: How to Drive Superior Results by Serving Others, Berrett-Koehler

Bailey, David H. and Borwein, Jonathan M., Why Are So Many Mathematicians Also Musicians? Huffpost, THE BLOG 05/03/2016 01:36 pm ET | Updated May 04, 2017

Bandura, Albert, 1997, Self-efficacy: The exercise of control,

Belsky, Scott, 2010, general partner for Benchmark Capital, published on http://99u.com/

BrainyQuote https://www.brainyquote.com/

Branden, Nathaniel, 1994, The Six Pillars of Self-Esteem, Bantam, New York

Brouwer, Paul J., 1964, The Power to See Ourselves, Harvard Business Review, no 64602, November-December

Brown, Brené, 2010, The gifts of Imperfection, Let go of Who You Think You're Supposed to Be and Embrace Who You Are, Hazelden

Butler, Richard J. and Gasson, Sarah L., 2006, Development of the Self-Image Profile for Adults, European Journal of Psychological Assessment, Vol 22(1): 52-58

Cooper, Edith, 2016, Success is Personal, Published on Influencer of LinkedIn, featured in: Career Development, Careers: Getting Started, Millennials, Productivity, Your Career, December 21

Dweck, Carol, 2014, How Companies can Profit from a "Growth Mindset", Harvard Business Review, November

Fein, Steven and Spencer, Steven J., 1997, Prejudice as Self-image Maintenance: Affirming the Self Through Derogating Others, Journal of Personality and Social Psychology, Vol. 73, No. 1, 31-44

Fuda, Peter and Badham, Richard, 2011, Fire, Snowball, Mask, Movie: How Leaders Spark and Sustain Change, Harvard Business Review, November

Habermacher, Andy, Ghadiri, Argang and Peters, Theo, 2013, You ain't got hope, if you ain't got SCOAP: the neuroscience of high-performing brains in business, Working Paper Nr. 1301, Version 3, Bonn-Rhein-Sieg University of Applied Sciences

Handy, Charles, 1999, Twenty-One Ideas for Managers: Practical Wisdom for Managing Your Company and Yourself, BBC Books 1990 / Penguin Books

Harvey, Steve, 2014, Act Like a Success, Think Like a Success: Discovering Your Gift and the Way to Life's Riches, Amistad, HarperCollins Publishers

Hill, Norman C., & Ritchie, J.B., 1977, The Effect of Self-Esteem on Leadership and Achievement: A Paradigm and a Review, Group & Organization Studies, December 1977, 2(4), 491-503

Ibarra, Herminia, 2015, The Authenticity Paradox, Harvard Business Review, January – February, pp. 52-59

Johari Window, http://kevan.org/johari

Karabell, Shellie, 2012, Leadership today: An inward journey, http://knowledge.insead.edu/leadership-organisations/leadership-today-an-inward-journey-582, April 26

Kets de Vries, Manfred, 2007, Putting leaders on the coach, Insead Knowledge, December 12

Krames, Jeffrey A., 2014, Lead with Humility, 12 Leadership Lessons from Pope Francis, AMACOM, a division of American Management Association

Leonard, Kelly and Yorton, Tom, 2015, Yes, And: How Improvisation Reverses "No, But" Thinking and Improves Creativity and Collaboration - Lessons from the Second City, HarperBusiness

Malley, Alex, 2014, The Naked CEO, The Truth You Need to Build a Big Life, John Wiley & Sons, Milton, Australia

McGraw, Phil, 2004, Self Matters, Create your life from the Inside Out, Pocket, UK

Neumann, J.E., 1999 & 2007, Class notes of the Practitioner Certificate in Consulting and Change, 2012-13, The Tavistock Institute of Human Relations

Pico, Jerry, 2015, On becoming self-aware, LinkedIn Pulse, August 2

PwC, 2015, The hidden talent: Ten ways to identify and retain transformational leaders, www.pwc.co.uk/human-resource-services

Rosh, Lisa and Offermann, Lynn, 2013, Be Yourself, but Carefully: How to be authentic without oversharing, Harvard Business Review, October

Schwartz, Tony, 2015, The Bad Behavior of Visionary Leaders, Life@Work in The New York Times, June 26

Snow, Shane, 2014, Smartcuts How Hackers, Innovators, and Icons Accelerate Success, Published by arrangement with HarperBusiness, an imprint of HarperCollins Publishers

Sunstein, Cass R., 2015, Choosing Not to Choose: Understanding the Value of Choice, Oxford UP

Swart, Tara, Chisholm, Kitty and Brown, Paul, 2015, Neuroscience for Leadership Harnessing the Brain Gain Advantage, Palgrave Macmillan, UK

Tjan, Anthony K., 2015, 5 Ways to Become More Self-Aware, Harvard Business Review, February 11, 2015

Tenney, Matt, 2014, Serve to Be Great Leadership Lessons from a Prison, a Monastery, and a Boardroom, John Wiley & Sons, Hoboken, New Jersey

Tracy, Brian, 2014, Leadership, AMACOM, American Management Association

Van der Walt, F. J. S. 1994, an Investigation into the strategic behavior of transformational Leaders, Graduate School of Business of the University of Stellenbosch in partial fulfillment of the requirements for the MBA

Weinstein, Bruce, 2015, The Good Ones, Ten Crucial Qualities of High Character Employees, New World Library, Novato, California

ABOUT THE AUTHOR

Flooris van der Walt is a clinical psychologist who practiced as a psychotherapist and is registered with the Health Professions Council in South Africa. In Switzerland, he is registered as a psychologist with the *Psychologieberufekommission* and is member of the Swiss Society for Coaching Psychology.

He received his post-graduate degree in Gifted Child Education, and subsequently completed an MBA, specializing in Human Resources. He enhanced this education with lifelong learning through courses including the *Advanced Human Resource Executive Program* at Michigan Ross Business School, *Human Resources in Asia* at INSEAD, *Entrepreneurship* at Babson College, *Senior Management Program* at IMD Business School, *Advanced Management Program* at Harvard Business School and *Consulting and Change* at the Tavistock Institute of Human Relations.

Today Flooris has his own business in Talent- and Organizational Development - vanderwalt GmbH (www.vanderwalt.ch)

www.ingramcontent.com/pod-product-compliance
Lightning Source LLC
Chambersburg PA
CBHW071208240526
45470CB00018B/1601